Agony of HELL

TURNER PUBLISHING COMPANY

TURNER PUBLISHING COMPANY

Author: W. Bert Craft

Turner Publishing Company's
Assistant Editor: Erik Parrent

Library of Congress
Catalog Card No. 94-060251
ISBN: 978-1-68162-125-8

Limited Edition

TABLE OF CONTENTS

AGONY OF HELL

W. Bert Craft

CHAPTER ONE
WORDS ABOUT THE AUTHOR

W. Bert Craft

The author was born in Smith County, Mississippi, on March 4, 1925. His parents were James William Craft, who married Cassie Ander Clark on February 28, 1909. James William Craft descended from the Cole and Hester families, while Cassie's ancestors were Clark, McGallion and Lee. Both parents claimed they were of Scotch-Irish descent and had a large family of nine children. Two sisters died shortly after birth, leaving seven living children, two boys and five girls. The children were reared on a small South Mississippi farm of 126 acres. James William Craft was a small time farmer and with the help of his wife, fed, clothed and educated their seven children solely from the products of the farm. Cotton was the money crop along with cucumbers, livestock, syrup, eggs, milk, butter and potatoes. Bread was made from corn, while meat consisted of beef, chicken, pork and occasionally wild game such as squirrels, rabbits, opossums and quail.

The children were given specific duties, such as milking cows, feeding the chickens, hogs, cattle, ducks and geese. Water was obtained by a windlass, drawing up two gallons of water each time from the well which was 108 feet deep. In addition to drawing water for personal use, water had to be drawn from this well for all of the livestock, chickens, etc. Fuel for cooking and heating came from cutting wood on the farm. Each child was assigned a specific chore, and unless there was a sickness the jobs were expected to be done daily. These chores were in addition to the farm work, which included plowing with mules, chopping and hoeing cotton and corn. In the fall, the cotton, corn, sugar cane, hay and sweet potatoes were harvested.

Fruits, such as peaches, figs, apples, pomegranates, as well as berries, were homegrown, picked and eaten. In addition, wild grapes and dewberries were plentiful. Watermelons, cantaloupes and musk melons were also cultivated.

James and Cassie were Christians and members of the Oak Grove Baptist Church, where they attended services regularly along with the children. All of the children were taught at home the love of God, family and country. They were also instructed to be proud of their country, state and the Confederacy, as both parent's grandparents, uncles and cousins fought for the South in the Civil War. James William Craft's maternal grandfather, John Marion Cole, fought with the Mississippi 46th Infantry Regiment, died at an old age, and was buried in the cemetery at the Jefferson Davis museum in Biloxi, Mississippi.

The writer still has the old powder horn, passed down through the generations. There is an interesting story about the powder horn. It was converted into a dinner horn and Cassie would call them from the fields by blowing from the horn. Even the working mules recognized what this sound meant. It was also used in the case of an accident or death to notify friends and neighbors of emergencies. Every time the kitchen was decorated, the horn was painted a new color. After James William Craft's death, it was given to me and I sanded it down to the original bone. I was amazed at the numerous colors of the rainbow that came off it.

CHAPTER TWO
CALL OF THE DRAFT

In the late 1930s, Germany and Japan were threatening war, and I, along with most of the other young boys, wanted to volunteer for duty, especially when we became 18. However, my parents advised me to graduate from high school and wait to be drafted. Complying with their wishes, I received my diploma from Mize High School, but the draft board prevented me from participating in the graduation exercise.

In late March of 1944, at the age 19, I received notice from the President of the United States to report to the draft board at the county seat, Raleigh, Mississippi, 20 miles northeast of my home. Our destination was Camp Shelby, Mississippi, 35 miles south of Mt. Olive where we were to take our physical examination; I passed it with flying colors. Being a shy country boy, I had never been undressed in front of an elderly person or a doctor before. In order to take the physical, all of us were lined up naked for the various exams (which were rather embarrassing to me and the others) and told to do some unusual things. It took three days for completion of the tests, and then we returned home. We called the school superintendent, C.H. Bradshaw, to request a one hour delay of the graduation exercises so we could attend, but he would not, and instead our diplomas were presented in absentia, much to the disappointment of our families, friends and loved ones.

Induction - Prelude To Basic Training

In the middle of April, 1944, I received notice to report to the draft board for the trip to the induction center at Camp Shelby. I reported as instructed about the 22nd day of the month. Again we were given tests, physical examinations, shots and interviews. The officer who interviewed me suggested that I select the Marines, because the Marines were more intelligent than the Army. I understood his viewpoint, but intuition told me that if I went into the Marines my service would be in the jungles of the South Pacific. I told him I would take the Army. My reasons were not divulged, but, personally, I preferred Europe over the South Pacific. He reluctantly assigned me to the Army.

On April 26, 1944, in the afternoon, we had been given GI clothes and were called out to be sworn into the service. We had no knowledge of how this was to be conducted. Thousands of us young recruits were marched into a huge auditorium. An officer appeared on the platform and spoke to us. After his speech, he told us to raise our right hand and repeat the oath. I resented this method, did not raise my hand, or recite the oath, as I felt this was an individual personal thing. By taking this action I did not consider myself unpatriotic, as I was perfectly willing and anxious to fight for my country. When the *Star Spangled Banner* was played and sung, a lump came in my throat and my eyes watered - and still does. No other song affected me in this manner except *Dixie,* the Confederate song.

We stayed in Camp Shelby for approximately a week, and the sergeant in charge of the barracks selected people at random to pull KP. Naturally, I was chosen and every morning would have to get up at 4 AM for duty all day. During the duration of this time, I had a serious case of tonsillitis, running a temperature, but being young and inexperienced, I would not go on sick call. I had almost a chronic case of this from early childhood until 1946, when my tonsils were removed. The Army doctors did not understand my plight, because sick call was early morning and they required one or two degrees of temperature before they would let a GI off duty. Along about 9 or 10 AM, my temperature would rise, but they did not care or were not aware of the disease.

We were told to assemble and get on a troop train but not told where we were going; that was Top Secret. Our destination turned out to be Anniston, Alabama, a short distance from Birmingham, Alabama.

CHAPTER THREE
BASIC TRAINING BEGINS

Upon arrival at Fort McClellan, we were greeted by a corporal who yelled all types of obscenities and called us "Mama's boys." After he finished speaking to us, an officer came out. We were supposed to stand at attention, but not knowing the Army rules, most of us did not, whereupon, we were immediately called "bastards," "sons-of-bitches" and every vulgar word he could think of - then the officer spoke. Someone asked the officer a question. By not prefacing his inquiry with a "Sir," this brought on another tirade of the same vulgar language.

We were assigned to temporary barracks as permanent ones for us had to be prepared. We really did not do anything but hold reveille and loaf for about a week. One evening I took a shower and my dog tags bothered me, as they did most of the boys. I, along with others, pulled them off and placed them on a shower wall. Naturally, the dog tags were forgotten and left in the latrine.

The next morning dog tag number 34988854 was called, and whomever it belonged to was supposed to identify it. Having not memorized the number, I did not respond. Before reveille was over, my name was called, along with others, and we were told to see the field sergeant. He asked me where my dog tags were; then it dawned on me where I had left them the night before, a mistake that cost me three days of extra duty.

From there we were assigned to Company A, 16th Battalion for basic training, where we had what I thought was a nice platoon sergeant. We were assigned rifles, bayonets and told to clean our equipment. My rifle was cleaned perfectly; I memorized my rifle number but overlooked cleaning the bayonet. Our sergeant had a notebook at inspection and put me on his "gig" list. The next day he was transferred to Officers Training School. The "gig" list was passed on to his replacement, a Sergeant Runnels from Missouri. This mistake cost me four or five weeks of extra KP and other duties, cleaning machine guns and other equipment. This guy, Runnels, was tough, but having become quite agitated and angry over the extra duty for so long, one day we came in from the field, and after calling out the "gig" list, which I was still on, he dismissed the platoon and headed for his quarters. I yelled out to him in front of the whole platoon, "Sergeant Runnels." He stopped and I went up to him and said in a loud voice, "Sergeant, I am getting damn tired of having to pull this extra duty for such a trivial thing as not cleaning my bayonet, when I did not know that it was a requirement in the first place, and I feel sure the previous sergeant did not intend to inflict this much harsh punishment for this length of time." He turned red and white, gritted his teeth, turned around and walked off. The other fellas followed me in the barracks and said, "Craft, you made a terrible mistake, in talking to the sergeant as you did." He will keep you on the gig list for the duration now." After I had cooled off a little, I realized this, but I put up a front and told them that at least I had gotten it off my chest. The sergeant apparently reconsidered, and I never pulled extra duty again. Nevertheless, if there was ever a horse's ass, he was a first class one.

During basic training, we were required to be up at 5:45 AM, dressed and have the beds made every day except Sunday for reveille. This was followed by chow, at the sound of the bugle, to eat the slop given us. Breakfast was usually the best meal of the day. During my early childhood years at home, mother always prepared fried eggs, well done, for all the family except Dad, who preferred his turned over lightly. The first breakfast we had fried eggs, cooked sunny side up. I asked the sergeant if mine could be well done and he let out a stream of cursing and told me I was getting the eggs as they were prepared - no exceptions; to go on my way and quit holding up the chow line. Having no choice but to accept this, I went on my way eating only the toast, jelly, coffee and a carton of milk. This happened several times, but usually there were never seconds on foods, so I was determined to eat what I thought was a raw egg. I developed a taste for fried eggs, sunny side up, and to this day, prefer them to be cooked in this manner.

During May, June, July and August, Fort McClellan seemed to be the hottest place on earth. On our first 10 mile hike, my shoes were one size too large, and I developed solid blisters on the bottom of both feet as well as on the sides and heels. The next morning my feet were so sore, that after chow, I went on sick call. I was not alone, one half of the company was there, too. I was called into a room for an interview with my platoon leader, a second lieutenant, who asked, "What is your trouble?" My response was that I had severe blisters on both feet, and they were so sore I could barely walk. His reply was, "Pull off your shoes and socks and let me see." I complied. He then reached on his desk, picked up a large needle and began to open the blisters, raked the large needle to drain all of the water out, and applied merthiolate to the blisters, which really burned. Then he added, "Get your shoes and socks on and report for duty." I don't remember this lieutenant's name, but he was a Spaniard who claimed to have fought in the Spanish Revolution, and he told us many fighting tales about the horrors of war.

I reported for duty as ordered, and we began with close order drill. Since my feet were so sore I had to walk on my toes, it was impossible to keep in step. In the 1st Squad I was the third man down the line, and I was keeping the whole squad out of step. Sergeant Runnels came back walking beside me and yelled at me to get in step. I told him my feet were solid blisters, and that

I could not. He said, "You damn softie, get to the rear of the squad." I did, and had to keep up in this fashion for several days.

At first, when we began training, we could not carry water in our canteens, but had to do without until noon; and in the afternoon, until we came in at night. We were told this would help us to do without water in combat. We did close order drill, went on marches, sat through classes on firearms, M-1 rifles, carbines, Browning automatics, machine guns, mortars, throwing grenades, using compasses, fighting mock battles and bayonet practices. A requirement was to tear an M-1 rifle down blindfolded and put it back together. We were allowed 10 minute breaks on the hour, read the articles of war, and had barracks inspection. If the inspector flipped a quarter on your bed and it did not bounce, you were gigged, given extra duty; if your foot locker was not packed properly, you got extra duty. If the hut, as a whole, did not please the inspector, all members of the hut were given extra duty. You were always required to know your service and rifle number. If asked and you did not know, it was extra duty.

It seemed like every morning some platoon sergeant was cursing his platoon with the obscene GI language. One particular morning the 3rd Platoon sergeant told his men how soft they were and that we had to go on bivouac; it required a 30 mile hike with full field packs, and we had to live out there in pup tents for several weeks. He referred to Baines Gap, which was a steep hill to climb, and said when we got to the bivouac area, there were numerous mosquitoes so large that they had intercourse with the wild turkeys. (Intercourse was expressed in the vulgar way).

I understand now that all of this harshness was their way of hardening us for combat. It was really tough on young 18 and 19 year old boys. It was even worse on the older men. We had a fellow named Egin, age 37, who had a pot belly and it was very difficult for him. We called him "Pop." By now I had grown up a lot and did not seek trouble, but I did not let any one push me around, either.

The first time I went to a movie, three or four of us who were buddies walked up to the ticket window. I asked for my ticket. I had barely beat a guy up to the window and he shoved me and the other boys out of the way and said, "I am a member of the Cadre, you cannot jump ahead of me." We let him get away with this, but this type of thing did not endear our hearts to the Cadre, both commissioned and non-commissioned officers.

We had to do this hard work, put up with this crap, and still retain our sanity.

Among other things, we had a physical training daily which included all types of exercise like running around a football field five times and doing at least 70 push-ups the Army way. If you failed to please the instructor, Second Lieutenant Mahaffey from Brooklyn, New York, you were required to run around the field five more times. He was a muscular man who was in real good physical shape and was very harsh, abusive and mean. I, along with many others, discussed shooting both Mahaffey and Runnels if we got into combat with them. Runnels became more abusive toward the end of our 17 weeks basic training. When our 10 minute break would come up, he would keep us at attention and walk off. The field sergeant would come up and dismiss us, and sometimes Runnels would come back and have the whole platoon standing at attention, thus depriving us of our break. I don't know to this day if this was made up between them or not, the field sergeant was a hard man, though he always seemed fair. Lieutenant Mahaffey was killed by the Germans in the Colmar Pocket; I don't know what happened to Runnels, but, as usual, the real tough guys in basic training, whether recruit or Cadre, did not perform as well in actual combat.

Toward the end of basic training, we were given a gas mask, put in a concrete building and gas was turned on. We were given extensive training on this as well as firing M-1 rifles, carbines, Browning automatics, machine guns, and 60 millimeter mortars. The M-1 rifle, because of the position and shape required to shoot it, was very difficult. I barely passed it. The first day I fired the M-1 rifle, it had a terrific kick and I sustained a large lump on the right corner of my lip. I don't know why, but even to this day, I am right-handed on everything else except shooting a rifle, shotgun or playing pool. It was always natural for me to do these three things left-handed.

Basic training was winding down, and they had officers from the Pentagon to observe. We first started out with close order drill, then unpacked our full field packs, displaying them on a blanket on the ground. Then we had an hour of physical exercise which included all the exercises, running around the football field five times, plus carrying a partner on our back across the football field, and he would return with you on his back. I got the raw deal on this as my partner was larger and heavier than I was.

We got a 10 minute break, packed our full field packs according to specifications. Our company was selected to do a speed march, five miles walking in step and running five minutes. We did this in 39 minutes which they told us was a record. The speed march was most difficult for me as my shin muscles had some sort of deficiency, and with my short legs, it was very difficult. As long as we were running I had no trouble, but I nearly caved in on the walking. Several times the corporal would come by and say, "Craft, there is no falling out; if you do, I'll bust your head in."

From there we were loaded on to trucks to the artillery field and had to simulate a battle with artillery exploding ahead of us. (Town Battles).

CHAPTER FOUR
TRAINING IS ENDING—LOOKING FORWARD TO HOME

In a simulated village fight we were given class instruction on the best ways to do house-to-house fighting. We had done the usual things of class, close order drill, physical exercise, etc. Then we were told to stack our rifles by squads. This was a unique process as the squad leader first selected a spot, stood his rifle straight up, the rest of the squad would use the hooks on their rifles and a perfect pyramid would form, and if everything was done correctly, they were right and would not fall. This, along with close order drill, was done constantly to prepare us for parades for the benefit of some general. The parades were performed for the generals quite frequently during basic and after the war. This was not only tiring, but distasteful, as we felt it was all for the whim of an officer.

Getting back to the village fighting, we were told another platoon had taken our rifles and we were to use theirs. We grabbed a rifle from the stack and proceeded to take the village. When I ran around to the rear of the first house, a large mud hole six or eight feet in diameter was close to the house and a member of the Cadre set off an explosive charge that sent mud flying up into the air at least 25 to 50 feet, and it came down on me and others, covering us with mud. We couldn't stop but had to finish the battle, proceeded on, and took possession of the village. Booby traps were on doors, and everything they could possibly think of that happened in battle, occurred. At the end of the day, we wearily marched back into the company area and after being dismissed, headed for the showers as all of us were tired, sweaty and very dirty. Since the rifles were mixed up, each one had to find his rifle; they all looked alike. The identification was the rifle serial number. A young man named Dan Dow, from Meridian, Mississippi, looked at the number on the rifle I had. He saw how muddy and filthy it was and told me in no uncertain terms that I had to clean the rifle as it was not in that condition when he left it in the stack. Apparently, he had not gotten the mud treatment I had. I informed him how it happened and that I had not yet found my rifle and did not know its condition; therefore, I did not feel any obligation to his rifle as mine, whenever I found it, would probably be in the same condition. He became belligerent, threatened to report me to the sergeant so that I would be ordered to clean it. By this time I had become angry, too, and I told him to report it to the sergeant. If I was ordered to clean the rifle, I would do so, but if this action occurred, he then should expect an ass beating because I did not intend to clean both his rifle and mine, too. He changed his mind and cleaned his own rifle. From that point on, our relationship was cool. He was discharged shortly before basic training was over.

Another situation we had was to crawl under barbed wire stretched tightly a length of 50 to 100 yards, in a very muddy area. Machine guns, using live ammunition, were firing over this area, and we were told that if we raised our heads we would probably be killed. This was a difficult thing to do as we had to also slide on our backs, keep our rifle on our stomach to keep it clean, and in firing order. This was a real ordeal and a test of courage. Fortunately, I accomplished this incident without as many problems as others had.

We had to scale a 12 foot wall and this created a hardship for me. To accomplish this, you had to run really fast for about 100 feet, throw your right foot up in order to bounce and lunge to the top. It took me several times, but I finally made it.

Another incident required was to go on a patrol with a compass at night and bring a squad back to an assembly place. The sergeant in charge of this selected me to be the patrol leader. I suppose he did not think I could do it, due to my small stature and baby face. As I did not have to shave, most of the guys referred to me as the "kid" except my close buddies. I led the patrol in the darkness through woods, across the hills, valleys, streams and was amazed that I got my men back to the assembly area in time.

During a simulated attack on a machine gun nest and shooting blanks, we were in an open field, water was standing on the ground, and I fell down in a dry place. The field sergeant came by me and said to me, "Craft, if that was a real machine gun firing, would you be where you are?" I said, "I don't see anywhere else to go for protection." He pointed to where a dual wheel truck had made deep ruts and I replied, "It is full of water." He shook his head and said, "If those were real bullets it would be your only chance, so roll over in the rut filled with water." I got wet and dirty, but later on in combat, this was a really good lesson. By this time, I was so sick of the Army and basic training, I thought I was ready for combat to get out of this mess. Again, perhaps, this was the basic training motive.

After that we were processed, given a 10 day delay-in-route furlough via our hometown to Fort Meade, Maryland. I enjoyed my few days at home. My parents were so pleased that I looked so well, they would not let me help with the harvesting. I had a good rest at home and knew that I was headed for Germany as an infantry replacement. Perhaps I should not have, but I told them from what I had heard and participated in, that they should not look for me to return, as it would take a miracle to survive infantry combat. Buford Lowery's father was kind enough to meet the train in Laurel, Mississippi and to take each one home, because we did not have transportation, and it was greatly appreciated. Buford had been a friend since we were in the first grade in school, and I considered him and his dear wife, Joyce, to be two of our closest friends.

CHAPTER FIVE
TRIP TO FORT MEADE, MARYLAND

My furlough had ended and it was now time to begin the journey to join a combat infantry division in France as a replacement. I previously failed to mention that I was inducted into the Army with quite a few close friends, Willard Clark, a distant cousin, together with a host of other Smith County young men. Also inducted at this time was Johnny Tillman Clayton, of Bethel Springs, Tennessee, staying with us through basic training and put in our infantry division. Incidentally, he was the last one of my old buddies who began with me, and was the last one of this group to be seriously wounded. That left me alone without a really close friend to finish the war.

In early September 1944, the final day at home, about 3:00 PM, Truett Thornton borrowed his brother's car and came by for me and talked with my family. Truett could sense my parent's despair and assured them that we would both return unharmed from the war. Little did he know; Truett was killed in the early part of November, 1944, and I was the only one to return to Smith County without being killed, captured or seriously wounded. Later I developed back trouble as a result of shrapnel.

We picked up some more boys at Mize and went on to Laurel, Mississippi, where we visited Truett's brother who lived there. He drove us to the railroad station to board our train at 6:00 PM. We rode this train three days and nights. The train was very crowded. All of us from Smith County were together again, raising cain and trying to be happy go lucky. Deep down in all of our hearts, we knew we were headed for hard times; but I know now that in our wildest imagination, no one knew (not having been there) the suffering, agony, and torment a combat infantry man went through.

We traveled through the mountains of Tennessee from the state of Mississippi. They were beautiful, and we stopped in Bristol. This is where I learned that the Main Street of town divided Tennessee and Virginia. We stayed on a side track for a while watching the people, then proceeded on to Baltimore. We transferred to another commuter train, mostly GIs, with a scattered number of civilians. All of us were seated, and the odd one from Smith County, a great big husky fellow, six and one half feet tall named Mac Thomas, was sitting in a seat by himself. A black man boarded the train and sat down beside him. Big Mac got red in the face and said, "Get up from here, Nigger. Where I come from we don't sit by Niggers." The black man became angry and yelled back at Mac, but decided to go somewhere else on the train. I don't know whether the black man knew it or not, but if he had hit Mac, he'd have had 25 or 30 Smith County guys who would have come to his aid. We went on to Fort Meade and were assigned to barracks two or three stories high. All of the hometown fellas stayed together, and also our friend, Johnny Clayton.

We were on the second floor and a slightly bald, red-headed, short young man named Anders was by himself. He was very friendly. In our conversation with him, we found out he had the Crabs. All of us liked the little guy, but were afraid of catching this pest, so in a very discreet manner, did not get too close to him, physically. Strange as it seems, this little fellow saved my life in combat which I will relate later in this writing. We stayed in Fort Meade a couple of weeks, falling out for reveille again at 5:45 each morning. It was very cold that year. We pulled light duty, went on a few hikes and speed marches, physicals, etc., but had a lot of free time.

The first weekend we went to Baltimore by rail and saw Sally Rand perform her strip tease act. The following weekend we went to Washington, DC and had dinner at a high class restaurant, which served alcoholic beverages. Naturally, we ordered one along with our dinner (Clark and Clayton were with me on this occasion). It was my second drink of liquor in my life and probably Clark's first; however, Clayton knew the ropes along this line better than we did. We fooled around later, looking at the sights and got on a bus in order to be back in camp by midnight. There was standing room only in the aisle, and I crawled up in the baggage compartment to keep from being pushed back and forth by the soldiers standing. Those standing envied me, because of my size I could do this and they couldn't. I went to sleep and asked them to wake me up when we got to camp.

The remainder of our spare time was spent seeing sights at or near the Fort, having our pictures made to send back home, and buying some small items. Among the things I bought was a Barlow pocket knife.

While at Fort Meade, Willard Clark, who was a very big fellow and had a very heavy beard, was continuously complaining about the GI razor he had and always borrowing mine. I had a nice safety razor that came with a kit given to me by my sister, Irene Barrett. I left the kit at home and carried the razor with me. Clark liked my razor so much, and since I didn't have anything but fuzz, one night I said to him, "I will make a deal with you. You keep my razor and I will use the GI one. When the war is over and we get back home, you can return it to me." He said that was fine with him, and it pleased him greatly. Things didn't work out that way though, he was killed the first day in combat and his personal items were sent home to his parents. When I visited them after the war, they showed me the personal things that were returned, and there was my razor, but I did not have the heart to tell them it belonged to me.

The speed marches were always difficult for me, as my legs around the shins became numb and this made it very arduous. After the war was over when we did the speed march, I found that going to the rear of the platoon and trotting did not bother my legs; neither did it hinder me in combat as I could go my own pace and, in spite of my stature and weight, assisted many of the larger fellows with their equipment, ammo., etc.

CHAPTER SIX
PORT OF EMBARKATION

Some time during the early part of the second week, we were transferred to the Port of Embarkation at Camp Kilmer, New Jersey, and that is where the secrecy began. We could not write home and use the Kilmer address. We were required to use an APO number. No long distance phone calls were allowed, and our mail was censored. While at Camp Kilmer we went to the movies and had a leisurely time. This lasted for about a week. It was rather enjoyable in spite of the uncertainty about where we were going. On the night of October 11, 1944, we boarded a train and got off at a railroad terminal near a seaport. It did not take a Philadelphia lawyer to determine this place was New York City. We boarded a ship single file, and some people handed each soldier a kit of some sort. They also gave us coffee and a donut. At first I thought this was the Red Cross, but later found out it was through the generosity of the Salvation Army.

Voyage To Europe

After being assigned to quarters down on Deck E, we found these to be large rooms with bunks stacked four or five high, and all the space between the rows was walking room only. All of us from Smith County were still together. True to form, I drew a top bunk. We were aboard the *Queen Mary*, second largest ship in the world at that time, owned and operated by the British. We were told there were 16,000 troops, not counting nurses and Air Corps officers. As usual, craps and poker games were continuously going on into the night, for the duration of the voyage. I did not participate in either of these games, as my parents would not have approved, and I felt it was a dreadful sin. It was told to me that one fellow finally came up the winner, winning several hundred thousand dollars. Food was prepared by the Limeys (British), and it was lousy.

At noon, October 12, 1944, several tug boats attached themselves to the big ship and began towing us out to sea. My close buddies Lowery, Clayton, Blackwell, Clark and others were fortunate enough to get on open deck and watch the Statue of Liberty fade into distance. I knew the purpose of the Statue meant freedom of speech, thought, and action for all, and still felt proud to fight for my country.

The *Queen Mary* traveled at a speed of 37 knots per hour and this meant probably 46 miles per hour. It did not require an escort as we were not in a convoy, and I did not experience any sea sickness, only a slight dizziness which did not last long at a time. At the time we boarded the ship, in an orientation period, we were informed there was no such thing as sea sickness and not to fraternize with the sailors, as they were more experienced in the ways of the world. The sailors were not allowed to enter our quarters or fraternize, either, as they knew all the tricks in poker and crap shooting and usually did not mix with soldiers, and riots broke out between the two groups.

The next morning about day break it seemed that every gun on the ship was firing. All of us jumped out of bed, dressed, ran up to the open deck. It was practically a riot as everyone had the same idea. We found out the gun crews were merely practicing. We thought we were being attacked by submarines, but were assured that a submarine or warship simply could not match the *Queen's* speed. We talked, loafed, walked around the ship, bought things from the PX and sometimes got lost on the ship. At times, we would go on open deck and watch the sea gulls and flying fish follow the ship and eat the scraps of food as they were thrown overboard. The weather was warm and clear.

One afternoon a Limey sailor came into our quarters and began to tell us about the horrors of war (he had fought in Africa and France) and that we would have it easy. As frightened as I was, it was never made known to my buddies or anyone, and I became bored with the sailor. Apparently I was smiling, for I recognized the fellow as a braggart and knew he was trying to impress us. He looked over at me and said, "Young man, you won't last long where you are going, and it won't take long to get that smile off your face." I, unlike my other friends, was not listening in awe and had grown weary of him, so I jumped up with my fist doubled and yelled, "You Limey son-of-a-bitch, I don't believe a word you are saying, you are not supposed to be down here anyway, and if you don't get out, I'll beat the hell out of you." The Limey turned white in the face and it was obvious that he was afraid, because he made a quick lunge for the door and disappeared with the laughter of the other GIs following him. Nothing unusual happened after that, and at daybreak on October 17, 1944, we landed in Glasgow, Scotland.

England And Across The Channel

When the anchors were dropped and the ship docked, we immediately got off and boarded a troop train waiting for us. The train was quite different than the ones in the States. It had compartments for four people with a table in the center, and we could play cards, talk, sleep, look at the countryside and discuss where we were going. Perhaps we went through the slums, for when we stopped, young children who looked ragged and undernourished would run up to the train begging for candy and food. We gave them all we had, but we did not have much ourselves. It really made us sad to see this type of thing. We rode all day and night, up to the next day to a Reple Deple (Replacement Depot) near Birmingham, England. After being assigned to barracks, we were again given orientation; that our stay was temporary, only a few days, and that we could not get passes to go into town. There had been too much trouble. From the officer's orientation, he explained no pass; to crawl through the wire and go to town was illegal and if caught, you would be court martialed. He also explained the reason white GIs could not go was that there were Negro troops who had access to the town, and when the whites saw a Negro with a white woman, usually a fight broke out, and the Limeys thinking the Negroes were American Indians would usually side with the Negroes; so we would not only be attacked by the local people, but would lose in a civil court and a court-martial. Being young boys, our curiosity was aroused and a bunch of us from Smith County went through the fence. We went into town, dodged the MPs and tried to talk to the local people. We found out we did not speak the same language as we could not communicate and since the MPs jeep got too close, we headed back to camp and remained there several days loafing. Again, we were put on a troop train, not knowing where we were going, and arrived in Southampton where we boarded a small troop ship and set sail for France. It took several hours. The ship could not go near the shore at Normandy; some LSTs picked us up and carried us as far as the water would permit. We had to get off and wade to shore from about 100 yards out. We were wet but led out to a pasture through mud, pitched tents and remained there for the night. In talking to some of the rear echelon stationed there, they informed us the invasion area where we were staying contained either a company or a battalion of Germans holed up in a pillbox that wouldn't surrender. The commanding officer in charge of that section ordered the bulldozers to cover it up. From all indications, this happened and the Germans perished by their own foolishness.

Another incident related to us about the invasion was that the Americans had encountered the Hedgerows. A German Tiger tank was holding up the American forces as our tanks were mounted with 75 millimeter guns while the German tanks with thicker armor carried an 88 millimeter gun. A Navy radio man was up front with the infantry and remarked, "I'll get the SOB" He took his map, located the enemy tank's position, and called back to his ship at sea which carried larger shells. The first round from the ship's guns got a direct hit, and our forces were able to advance.

The next day it was raining, and we packed our packs, were loaded in trucks, and headed toward the front lines. This was a situation where it took several days. Again, I wound up on the short end. They loaded us on the truck by the alphabet, and it fell my lot to have to sit in a seat made by stacking the field packs in the center. Somehow, this Private Haney, whom I first saw at the Reple Deple, was a very tall fellow who looked belligerent at times when he wasn't even mad, and he seemed always to be looking for a fight.

We had to sit straddling the seat made by the field packs. Haney was seated against the cab. Whenever the truck would stop, the load of eight people came crushing down on me, pushing me into Haney, pressing him against the cab. He would push back on me with his hands, then beat my back, complaining to me it was all my fault. I put up with this all day into the afternoon, and we would stop in various towns waiting for someone else to move out up ahead. I don't know what caused the traffic jam, but the Frenchmen in the western part of France were very friendly and happy to see us. They brought us all sorts of things while the convoy was at a standstill, such as, apples, apple cider, wine and cognac. We graciously accepted all of these gifts. They gave us several bottles for the truck since there were probably 24 people on each vehicle. We were rather crowded and when Haney got the wine and cognac, he drank more than his share, that's the kind of person he was. I took a couple of drinks when it was passed around, and because I never had drank before, it made me feel really good. I got tired of Haney pushing on me, and I asked the fellow on the side seat to swap. Haney had made such a pig of himself drinking cognac, that he got sick and vomited on the guy next to me on the side seat. I remarked to this fellow saying, "I wouldn't let him get away with that if I were you." Haney replied, "You little son-of-a-bitch." As soon as that came out of his mouth, I slugged him in the face with my fist. That shut him up for the rest of the trip until that night when we stopped to sleep out in a field alongside of the highway.

The reason for my violent reaction was, back home in Smith County, when a person called another a son-of-a-bitch, it meant that his mother was a whore, prostitute, or to say the least, frequented other men's beds. I loved and cherished my mother dearly and this was the reason for my reaction.

When the convoy pulled off the road onto the field, we were told to unload, and it was more convenient for the boys sitting straddle on the field packs to get out first. The middle row scooted along the makeshift seat getting out of the truck, and Haney slid along the seat by me and stopped in front of W.C. Blackwell, one of my school mates, and said to him how sorry he was for the disturbance he had caused. Blackwell told him, "It's quite all right. You haven't offended me," but Haney kept insisting on apologizing and held out his right hand as if to shake, but suddenly withdrew his hand, doubled his fist and struck me under the chin, knocking my head against the post that held the canvas top secure. He really hit me hard and, momentarily, I actually saw bright stars twinkling. In being prepared to exit from the truck, I had my steel helmet with the liner inside of it and was holding it between my legs top side out. I was clutching the helmet with both hands and my instant reaction was to strike back with the helmet, using all the strength I could muster, hitting Haney in the face, as he was leaning towards me. My blow with the helmet literally lifted him up and backwards, screaming in pain. I immediately jumped on top of him and started hitting him in the face with my fist.

He was yelling and trying to get a knife from his pocket. Willard Clark noted this and said, "Bert, get off him and out of the truck. He's going to knife you." Clark, Thornton and Blackwell pulled me off him and shoved me out of the truck. All three of them were well over six feet tall and probably weighed about 200 hundred pounds. As I landed on the ground, my friend Eads from Alabama was standing at the rear of the truck and had his knife out with a long blade. He, too, was feeling good from the cognac and thought that Haney was hurting me. He was really angry and he called Haney every vulgar name in the GI language, and also told him, "If you hurt the kid, I'll cut your heart out."

He was inviting Haney to come on out, but Haney was afraid to come out. As Eads attempted to climb into the truck, I grabbed hold of him and told him that everything was all right as I had beaten the hell out of Haney. That stopped him, but he told Haney that he was an overbearing bully and if he ever hurt the kid, referring to me, that he would kill him. Clark, Blackwell and Thornton also told Haney that he would have to account to them if he ever bothered me again. However, as long as we remained together, I usually found one of the three with me and believe to this day that they were self-appointed body guards as Haney had said he would get revenge.

The next morning I saw Haney. His face looked horrible, and he had a huge knot under his left eye. From then on, he avoided me, probably because he knew I had too many friends, nevertheless, I too, kept my eyes open as I did not intend to take a beating from him.

We got back on the trucks and rode all day to another Reple Deple (Replacement Depot) near the front lines where we could hear our own artillery firing. This was frightening as we knew shortly, we too, would be on the front lines facing the enemy. This was near Epinal, France, and we stayed there for a couple of days in big tents.

One afternoon they called our names again alphabetically, and told us we were assigned to the 3rd Infantry Division. We immediately boarded trucks and by mid-afternoon arrived at Division Headquarters.

CHAPTER SEVEN
ENTERING COMBAT

Division Headquarters was located in a huge apartment complex. We unloaded and were told the Division Commander would speak to us. A short, squatty man with a stern look on his face got on the platform and introduced himself as General Mike Grafton. He had a deep gruff voice and welcomed us to the 3rd Division, known also as the Marne Division. The division had performed in World War I on the River Marne and had successfully defeated the Germans, getting a high medal with much honor. He also informed us the division had started in Africa, Sicily, Italy (Anzio Beachhead), invaded Southern France and had an excellent record in World War II, and he expected us to continue this record by killing the Bosch (Germans). His manner of speaking, the things he said reflected hatred of the Bosch, killing them and removing Nazi tyranny from the face of the earth. He further stated that we were expected to be tough, as the division had a superior record which would be upheld. The division had never retreated under any circumstances and his job was to see that we killed the Bosch.

While I cannot recall his exact words, he was inspiring us to go into our assigned units and do our duty to win the war. My first impression of this man was he was cruel and mean, not caring about his men. When in reality, he was trying in his position to inspire us to go out and perform as good soldiers. He had his own Piper Cub (plane) and whenever possible, he would fly over us during the fighting. At the end of the Colmar Pocket, he drove through our battalion, congratulating us on a job well done. During my service with the division, I had mixed feelings about him, admiration for his accomplishments, and disgust over the hardships and terror we underwent. Most of my comrades felt that he wanted to become famous and build a name for himself by volunteering our division for tougher battles, which we might not have undergone if left to the discretion of the 7th Army.

When he completed his speech, he abruptly left and our names were called alphabetically and assigned to regiments. Anders, W.C. Blackwell, Doc Boykin, Willard Clark, Johnny Clayton, myself, Eads, Haney, Buford Lowery and J.B. Thompson were assigned to the 7th Infantry. J.B. Thornton and Truett Thornton were assigned to the 15th Infantry Regiment and Mac Thomas was assigned to the 30th Infantry Regiment. We were officially in the 3rd Division on October 29, 1944, and were assigned to our regiments on November 1, 1944. It had taken only 17 days from the time we left New York harbor to reach the front.

Joining the 7th Regiment and Engaging in the Battle of the Crossroads of Hell

We again were loaded on trucks to join the 7th Regiment. It happened so swiftly that we waved goodbye to our friends who were going in separate directions. Those assigned to the 7th Regiment were dumped in a pasture with groves of evergreen trees and heavy foliage to conceal us. The information as to our location or what was going on was not given to anyone. We spent two days and nights wondering where we were going. Anders, Blackwell, Boykin, Clark, Clayton, Eads and myself were assigned to the 1st Battalion. Lowery and Haney were assigned to the 2nd Battalion, and I don't recall where the others went.

It was beginning to get really cold, and our quarters were pup tents that night. We awakened the next morning to a cold drizzle of rain. Deciding to build a fire, we sought out dead twigs and wood. Because the twigs were wet, it was difficult to get a fire started. I pulled my new Barlow knife out of my pocket and began to whittle shavings from the twigs. The twigs were very hard; my right hand slipped and a piece of the twig went under my right thumb nail. My immediate reaction was to pull it out and, though my thumb was hurting, I assisted in building a fire to keep warm.

It seemed like our group was getting smaller as replacements were being taken to their respective battalions as safety would permit. The first battalion replacements were the last to leave as they were engaged in a fierce battle. On the fourth day of November, near mid-afternoon, we were put in jeeps and headed up a mountain road, then we got off and proceeded up a trail where we came upon a group of GIs and a jeep in the middle of a trail with a dead German lying across the hood, wrapped in a blanket. The Krauts either saw us or were shelling at random, because the shells began dropping in. The person in charge yelled for us to dig in.

This was a terrible chore near the base of this rocky mountain. Our fox holes were dug and after the shelling, no one was injured. We were told to move out. Continuing a few hundred yards, the shelling began again, and we were told to dig in. Clark, Clayton, Eads and myself did not put our hearts into this second fox hole; we played around with it and as we had ascertained, were told to move on and arrived at a small cliff in the mountain. Roll call again was called, putting Clark and Clayton into Charlie Company 1st Platoon with Eads and myself into the 2nd Platoon. Clayton spoke up to the sergeant in charge and requested that he assign Clark and Craft to the 1st Platoon and assign him to 2nd Platoon, because Clark and I were from the same hometown. The one in charge agreed and assigned us accordingly.

From there we caught hold of a rope and pulled ourselves up the small cliff to the top where Charlie Company was attempting to knock out a machine gun nest. Much to our surprise, we saw heavy-bearded, long-haired, dirty, filthy figures who, upon close examination, turned out to be human (GIs). We saw a big tall guy, who was Mel Atney, stand up and yell, "Go get the son-of-a-bitch who was spraying the whole area with machine gun fire." We were not organized, but advanced toward the machine gun and were stopped by concertina wire, which is nothing more than barbed wire, rolled about two or three feet high. We stopped there and began firing. I could not get off a good shot, however, Clark did, and the machine gun quit firing as darkness had set in. We were told to dig in. Clark and I were foxhole buddies and selected a spot under a huge tree. By working really hard, we managed to dig a hole about six feet long and six inches deep. It was not adequate, but the stones and roots were too much, so we quit. In situations like this, one could sleep, while the other pulled guard. Clark and I alternated turns throughout the long night; he appeared to sleep some, however, I did not close my eyes. Artillery and mortar shells exploded continuously all night long, wounding and taking its toll of lives. A German was screaming in pain way into the night. It was a pitiful wail; no one cared or dared to help him as it could have been a trap. While I was sitting up pulling guard that night, an 88 shell hit the top of the tree and fell on the other side without exploding. Morning came. It was cold and everyone was tired and sleepy. We ate a K-Ration breakfast, and I told Clark about the shell that was a dud (did not explode). We looked around on the other side and found it not daring to touch it, because they were known to explode if disturbed or moved. By that time Mother Nature called and it was time for a bowel movement. I pulled down my trousers, used twigs and leaves for toilet tissue since there was none available, covering waste excretion with dirt and leaves.

By that time we were called upon to get moving, as the company was getting ready to move out in the attack. The Germans had retreated to new positions and we headed out single file. The 1st Platoon was in reserve, Pinski and Tort were the scouts. The company had suffered such severe casualties that there were only six men in our platoon; however, before we moved out, a clean-shaven sergeant joined us from rest camp. His name was Troy White from Tennessee. He was looking at how many men we had. Then looking down at me, he stared. A smile appeared on his face and he said, "Good God, is it really that bad back in the States?" Addressing me, he asked, "Son, how long have you been weaned from your mother's breast? You don't appear to be a combat soldiers' age." I replied, "Sergeant, I am 19 years old, but if you will put that in writing and it will get me back to the States, it will suit me." He chuckled and said, "Let's get moving."

Pinski and Tort suggested Clark and I should be scouts, but White said, "No, not today. Let's give them a little experience." We moved out going down the mountain, then climbed another one. Around noon a runner came back from the company commander and needed two men to go on a contact patrol, as we had lost radio contact with B Company. White ordered Clark and I to go on patrol with four other men. Our instructions were to veer off to the left and "you will find them." Anyhow, we walked several hundred yards to our left and we came to a clearing. We saw a group of men down, about a 100 yards away at the other side of the clearing. They appeared to have on GI clothes; we thought it was B Company and yelled out to them, but they wouldn't answer. One of our men threw up his rifle and started shooting over them. When he shot his rifle, we found out they were Germans. They started cursing us in German and ran and got their guns and opened up on us with machine guns. We retreated into a clump of bushes to hide. Fortunately, I got behind the largest tree I could find. It was huge and it hid my body, but Clark got behind a little tree and those older experienced fellows retreated 10 to 15 feet behind us. Clark and I were closer to the Germans than they were.

The Krauts began to shell us with mortars and bullets were flying all around us. They lightened up on the shooting and we could hear the Germans walking in the leaves trying to get us to come out. We wouldn't say anything. There was a little road or path we had walked down to our present position from the other direction. I looked up and saw a German. Apparently, he must have been SS who had on this black uniform and he looked awesome. I got off one shot and either got him or missed him — I don't know which. I only know he fell on his face and did not get up.

The Krauts apparently spotted Willard Clark. They sent several bursts of an automatic weapon and he began to roll over and over, turning somersaults with the big cumbersome heavy pack on his back. I was afraid he might choke or break his neck, so I crawled out to him under fire to pull him back and attempt to give any aid possible. By the time I reached him, I knew he was dead. Using my Barlow knife, I cut the pack straps and laid his head upon it. This was a terrible experience for me as I was frightened and angry.

We looked up and saw GIs coming between us and the Germans. We headed back looking for Charlie Company and found them. When we found C Company, they had six prisoners. They had built a fire and the prisoners were warming their hands. When I saw those Germans it infuriated me. I threw up my gun to shoot them, but a guy by the name of Pinsky reached over and pulled my gun down saying: "Don't shoot 'em here, buddy. They need it, but they'll court—martial you for that and shoot you if you kill them in cold blood." I said, "Yeah, but those dirty son of a bitches just killed my buddy from back home, who was on the patrol with me." He answered, "I understand. They need shooting but don't do it." I reluctantly put my gun down by my side, and stared at those Krauts. I really wanted to get them. We stayed there for a while and then were ordered to move. Before we pulled out, Johnny Clayton came over to tell me that when they had gotten to this place Eads was first scout and Johnny was second scout, 2nd Platoon. A German stepped from behind a tree and shot Eads in the head. He whirled around to get Johnny and Johnny pulled his gun quicker and shot him, killing him stone dead.

Anyway, shortly thereafter, we were told we had to move out. We moved a short distance and were going down the hill and a German came crying out of the bushes. Everybody hollered, "Don't shoot them. Give them a chance to surrender. There are probably some more." Some four, five or six more came and were taken prisoner. Apparently this was reported to Battalion Company Commander, who told us to hold there. We put out a perimeter guard — it so happened the 1st Platoon was at the rear end of the line and this young man, who was supposed to contact me, apparently went to sleep on the job, because he let the other fellow go off and leave him, and there were about six or eight of us lost. We looked around and saw that everybody was gone. We didn't know which direction they had gone, not having a radio, we didn't know what to do. We decided the best plan was to go down the mountain trail straight ahead. We proceeded in this manner and got so close to the Germans we could hear them.

After a conference, we decided it would be better to go back to the trail crossroads. We went back up there and spent the night. Everyone had colds and being real close to the Germans, we didn't want them to know where we were. Everybody was suppressing their cough by pressing their adam's apple. We had this one guy that didn't keep the proper contact and got us into this predicament. He coughed all night long. We threatened to shoot him and called him every kind of name in the GI language. Still his old hacking cough persisted. We didn't sleep much that night. The Germans were not shelling us. Apparently they didn't think we were that close to them, but we could hear the big stuff — our big 155s. They were shooting over this mountain down into the town, Taintrux. They were shooting at a Kraut roadblock and other enemy positions. Those shells didn't have far to go from where we were, and apparently they were arched over this mountain whining over us. We could almost reach up and touch them. It was a strange, weird feeling — lost at night near the enemy with all those shells swishing overhead.

The next morning we decided to go back down the same trail. We got part of the way down and captured a German, then decided to go back to our original position. We went back up there and saw Captain Rock, B Company, CO. He was out on reconnaissance himself and we asked him Charlie Company's location as we were lost. He said, "It's down that trail to the right, only a short distance from here." Boy, were we glad to see him and were we happy to get the information! We found our company, they were off this trail dug in. Sergeant White was really glad to see us. He told us to dig in. No sooner had we dug in; it started raining.

In the meantime, artillery could be heard exploding. We could hear machine guns and rifle fire, and we were ordered to go into attack. After it started raining, we had to get some twigs and limbs off the trees. Evergreen trees, I think. Like some of those we have out west in the States. Anyway, they were like pine trees that you could use to build a little shelter. We got into company formation. I believe the 1st Platoon and maybe the 2nd Platoon were leading, and the other platoons were following. We got down pretty close to a paved road on the side of a mountain and the Germans opened up on us. We attempted to shoot it out with them, but didn't seem to be getting anywhere. Old Pinski, the first scout from my platoon, wanted to crawl up close and throw a grenade into the enemy machine gun nest, but Haney, an officer, wouldn't allow it. Like any fight where bullets were flying, it was dreadful, but the most frightening were the soldiers' screams of pain when they were wounded. We retreated, carrying our wounded with us. I often wondered (I was never told), but believe we were sent down there to find out what was there; because after we got back, the artillery gave it a lambasting that persisted pretty well all through the night. We returned to the foxholes where we had dug in and which provided a little shelter with the evergreen tree limbs. We stayed there through the night.

They told us rations were down on the paved road and wire was strung to where they were. There was a jeep and some trucks down there. I was selected from my platoon with Tort, my buddy, to go down and pick up the rations. We got a hold of the wire and followed it in the darkness. We were cautioned that the Germans might come in and cut the wire and lead it to their place so they could easily capture us. Our hearts were in our mouth, at least mine was, walking down this mountain, being so dark you couldn't see in front of you. This wire went through underbrush and curved around trees. We took a beating from being hit with limbs stumbling and falling. Tort and I finally made it down. When we arrived, we found an open body truck. The small truck was full of bread and was stacked in rows. Immediately Tort and I grabbed a loaf of bread, tearing the crust off and dug in the middle eating like dogs. There was no water. We got the rations for our platoon. In the meantime, Johnny Clayton came down for his platoon and we began talking. He was telling me a little bit about what he had heard — that Blackwell and Boykin had gotten hit. We didn't have much time to talk, got our rations together and headed up the mountain. Fortunately, the Germans hadn't bothered our wire, because we came back to our company area.

We ate without water or coffee. Then White sent Pinski and another guy to get water. They knew where a river was. They came back. We were all thirsty. We couldn't wash or shave, but at least had enough water to drink and make coffee. I must have drank a full canteen and a couple of refills. The Pollock, Pinsky, had a weird sense of humor. He said, "We went down and found this little mountain stream, knelt down and drank all we could hold. We filled two five gallon cans and as we started to walk back up stream, we saw a dead German deteriorating in the water." Apparently, his motive was to make us sick or disgusted, but he did not fool me as he did the others. Being reared on the farm, I knew water purified itself at a certain distance, so I began to question him about how far it was. He said, "50 or 100 feet." I replied, "The water is good, because water purifies itself after running that far." That killed his joke. Everybody was satisfied and felt better with my explanation. We stayed there that night. It was misty rain, but the tree limbs gave us some protection. However, it was very cold and uncomfortable. Being fresh from the States, we had full field packs with us and used those tents to help out. We didn't really set up a tent, we spread them over us. The ones that had those fared better than the older guys that didn't have tents.

Early the next morning, at the crack of dawn, we were up, ready to move out. They didn't tell us where we were going. We went in the same direction that we did the day before. When we got down there, apparently the artillery had done its job, because no Germans were in sight. The battle patrol was with us. Going by the same place that we had fought the day before, we saw this elaborate road blockade. In preparing their defense, the Krauts had used forced labor to cut trees that extended all the way across the road so you couldn't possibly drive around it. They had four of those trees sunk into the ground on each side of the road, then stacked poles in between creating a wall 10 to 12 feet high. It couldn't be scaled very easily; you couldn't go around it. You had to knock the enemy out which was fortified with infantry, tanks, mortars and large guns. We saw the foxholes where the Germans were defending this road-block, and they really had it set up where they could cover everything. They could cover coming up or down the road or from either side. We went on through it cautiously and came to the edge of Taintrux. Approaching a farm house, we knocked on the door and six Germans came out with their helmets off and hands over their heads, surrendering. We were getting ready to send them off and the Germans said something to the French woman. Would you believe that the Frenchman and his wife went up to each of those Germans and hugged and kissed them on each cheek? That was so disgusting to us that we felt like shooting them. But, nevertheless, that brought us into Taintrux, where we were to stay a day or two.

Built onto their house was their barn. You could walk right out into the barn from the kitchen. They had a few chickens, horses, cows and a good supply of hay. Tort and I were to guard the barn door. We were to sleep in

CHAPTER EIGHT
REST AND REHABILITATION

Finally, on November 9, 1944, we were informed that we were to be relieved by the 103rd Division, and that we were going back to take some river crossing training.

The morning of the 10th, apparently, they had moved the 103rd Division, or one of their regiments up to replace us. The 103rd was new from the States, and they hadn't yet had the baptism of combat. They came up on the mountain at night and on the morning of the 10th, their stupid officers required them to have reveille. Everything had quieted down and at 6:00 AM the bugle began blowing. Even a rookie like me, merely being on the lines seven days, knew this was sheer foolishness. It was stupidity, because when the boy played reveille, we had a vivid picture of those poor guys hauling up and getting into formation, but the Krauts knew what to do. They knew where the sound was and immediately the 103rd was bombarded with artillery. What could we do? We felt foolish even though we weren't doing it ourselves. Some choice comments were made about how stupid having reveille on the front lines was and the bad judgment on the part of the dumb officers. The officers thought they were of superior intellect. They referred to themselves as "officers" and we were called "men." This always went against the grain as far as I was concerned, because I felt like I was just as good as they were, but as Army rules were, I had to obey them, or make the appearance of obeying them, anyway. We knew it had to be officer's stupidity, which was repeated many times.

At dark on November 10, 1944, they moved us out by trucks. We drove for a long way, far into the night, arriving at the assembly areas in the vicinity of Fremifontaine and Pierrepont, France. This move was made without incident. The period of offensive combat from October 20 to November 10, 1944, was the stiffest the regiment had encountered in France up to that time. An important part of La Mortagne River Valley and its tributaries had been wrested from the enemy. About 10 miles of rugged terrain, covered by dense forest, had been traversed over the face of the most determined resistance. The "COTTON BALERS" had fought gallantly and courageously in some of the roughest fighting of the French campaign. "Cotton Balers" or 7th Infantry Regiment earned this name in the battle against the British. This was the Battle of New Orleans, where cotton bales were used as breastworks. This battle was fought under the leadership of Andrew Jackson on January 8, 1815.

There were 1,086 Germans that had been processed through the regimental POW cage, while numerous others were evacuated through medical channels. A great many of the enemy had been killed, much equipment destroyed and captured. The regiment suffered its losses in obtaining its objectives. There were 148 "Cotton Balers" that had sacrificed their lives. Two of these were Willard Clark and Lee L. Eads. There were 822 who were wounded and evacuated. Two of these were W.C. Blackwell and Doc Boykin. We moved by trucks. We got off the trucks in the assembly area in a large pasture, with a scattering of evergreen trees on it. Large tents had been set up for us — 10 to 15 men could occupy these tents. There was a shortage of sleeping bags. It was beginning to get cold, and Tort and I slept in the same sleeping bag. It was a wonderful feeling to be back off the lines, not having to pull guard or worrying about being shot. I woke up early the next morning, my kidneys had to act, and I needed to go to the bathroom, but I didn't know where the latrine was. They had field latrines for us. For that many men it was necessary. I continued twisting and turning. It made Tort mad and he cursed me out and said, "Get up and go piss and quit moving so much. I'm sleepy." Finally Tort said, "Since you won't be still, let's both go piss." We found the field latrine. It was an open ditch to be used for this purpose. Needless to say, I was very much relieved. Then, we walked from there to the field kitchen. By that time chow was ready, and believe me, we had some of the best cooks, I believe, or else after not having chow for 10 days and just eating cold food, it was welcome. We didn't even have perked coffee in combat; we only heated water and used instant coffee. I have a hatred of instant coffee to this day, because of having to drink it in combat. We used our canteen cup and put in it a little bag of instant coffee. To heat our coffee, we had a little combustible pill that would burn. You could light it with a match or cigarette lighter and it would catch fire. It was large enough and would burn long enough to heat a cup of coffee. We heated our coffee by using our canteen cup and putting a little bag of instant coffee in it. We had plenty of coffee and sugar. There's no question about that.

We all learned to have our pockets full of coffee, sugar, cigarettes and candy. The sugar and coffee came in small packets. If nothing else, we always managed to have coffee and water. That seemed to be essential as far as our eating was concerned, because you couldn't carry bulky rations. It was very difficult to carry food with all your ammunition. Tort and I got to the temporary mess hall that was set up, and a line was formed. People were shaving and heating water. Those guys (their beards were at least an inch long) and they looked like wild men. You know in looking back today, when we have these fellas going around with heavy beards and long hair, well, you see, this was displayed in combat, which we detested tremendously, because we were in the short hair era. The long hair and heavy beards were always dirty and unclean. Nevertheless, some of them were shaving before they ate or had gotten up early and had shaved. Tort and I hit the chow line first. And, boy, I'm telling you, they had hot cakes, and we filled our mess kits full of them. We got six to eight in a serving. They made their own syrup and had bacon by the bushel. The food was piping hot and delicious. The cooks would pop down six or eight pancakes on a mess kit, reach over and get a handful of bacon. They didn't count pieces, giving each man six or eight slices, realizing we were hungry. They put the bacon on top of the hot cakes, then reached over and got a dipper full of syrup. They were very generous in their servings of the syrup, because they poured it over hot cakes and bacon and you had plenty of syrup at the bottom. We got our coffee, went back and devoured it like hungry dogs, then got back in the chow line again. I really don't know how much we ate, it was so delicious. There was no limitation on what you could eat, because the cooks knew that we had not had hot chow in a long time.

After everybody was given time to shave, etc., we were called out for company assembly to check the roll. A list of names of people who had been killed was read. The first sergeant said he would call out the names of the dead. If anyone knew the exact location of the bodies, they would be taken to the general vicinity by the members of the Graves Registration people. It would be helpful to them to have someone who knew to point out the spot. Willard Clark and Lee Eads' names were called along with many others. When asked if anybody knew, I told Sergeant White I did, and he said, "Yeah, we have somebody." He went on down the list and called the rest of the remaining names. When they got to Eads, Johnny Clayton said he did. We were asked to see the first sergeant who said to us, "If you two guys will, go with these fellas from the Grave Department. They'll take you pretty close to the general vicinity, then you can show them the exact spot where they were killed, and they won't have to hunt for the bodies. "

We got in the truck, riding in the back. The two men with the Grave Registration were in front. We went to a mountain and left the truck at the bottom of the mountain and walked up, coming to Eads' body first. Johnny Clayton found it. Johnny showed us exactly how Eads was killed. It was where a Kraut had stepped out from behind the tree Eads had walked past, and the German shot him behind the ear, killing him instantly. The dead Nazi was also there where Johnny had shot him. It was too much for two men to carry the dead bodies. They had a haver sack that was part of a tent, placed the body on it, and dragged it down to the truck. Incidentally, I failed to mention it had snowed that night, the first night we were there. We woke up to a light snow, about two or three inches on the ground. You can visualize how cold it was, the bodies were covered with snow. One of the grave bearers dragged Eads' body back down to the truck. The other one, with Johnny and I, went to find Willard Clark's body. There he was, like I'd left him. I had taken his head and placed it upon his pack. He was covered with snow. We uncovered him, put him on a haver sack, and the grave bearer in charge dragged him down the mountain through the snow, and put him in back of the pickup truck. This method of retrieving our friends' bodies made Johnny and I both unhappy. We picked up some more bodies, but one of them was a most "interesting" story.

It seems that before we joined the outfit, Charlie Company was in a fight and a Captain Cocke had joined "C" Company as company commander. They had dug in and, as I have mentioned before, digging foxholes on that mountain was a serious matter. It was a very difficult thing to do. There were some places you couldn't dig. This is what happened, and the physical evidence we saw vividly portrayed the situation. We saw all those foxholes, with several dead bodies in them. In one particular foxhole there were two bodies within. One of the bodies had captain bars on it. We saw his helmet and another soldier's body with it. We were told the captain looked down and saw this nice foxhole that two other GIs had dug. He pulled rank, being "Mr. Captain," not even a man, a superior. He ordered them out of the foxhole and took it over along with his orderly. Perhaps it's better not to comment on this, but the story will speak for itself. Shortly after they took over the foxhole, a German mortar got a direct hit on the foxhole killing both the captain and his orderly. The two boys he chased out, who did not have a foxhole, came out of the battle without a scratch. This story was told to us by the two men we were assisting. Later on, after the war, this story was verified by Sergeant White.

By the time we were through collecting all the bodies pulled them down the mountainside stacked them into the truck, it was fully loaded. The cab of this truck being small, we had to ride in the back with the corpses, and frankly, had to sit on them. We drove for an hour or two and came to Grave Headquarters. They had an area sealed off by a fence, and the dead bodies were stacked like cord wood. One of those fellas began to search the bodies and take out information. He pulled out Willard Clark's billfold and looked at the contents, including the pictures. He looked at Willard's wife and said, "Oh boy, could I go for her!" and he could not stop admiring her. I took it as long as I could, then said, "Look, you son-of-a-bitch, you better put that picture and all his belongings up and make your record, but don't you ever speak disparagingly of this woman, because this dead man is my friend from my hometown and if you don't shut up, I'll shoot you." He was frightened because I had my rifle and quickly made records. We disposed of all the bodies and went on back into the bivouac area. I don't know how far we were from this area, because we spent most of the day doing this job. It must have been a pretty good distance behind the lines. This was one of the most painful experiences of my life.

We drove on back to camp amd went to bed. All during the night, my right thumb started throbbing and hurting. It was infected. A day or two before I joined the outfit, I was building a fire with a new Barlow knife (purchased in Fort Meade, Maryland) when my knife slipped and a twig went up under my thumb nail. I pulled part of it out and thought I had gotten it all, but I hadn't. The next morning I had red streaks running up my arm and Sergeant White told me, "You better go and get something done for your thumb." I went to the Aid Station. A doctor looked at it, got a gleam in his eye, raised the thumb nail up, put some tweezers underneath the nail, and pulled the rest of the splinter out. He put some more alcohol on it and swabbed it with merthiolate. He gave me some sulphur pills and told me not to pull any duty.

CHAPTER NINE
CROSSING THE MEURTHE RIVER

While my outfit was taking training to cross the Meurthe River, which was to be our next objective, I stayed in the bivouac area and loafed and rested. However, I didn't get any of the details on what we were to do or how we were to do it. I doubt if I missed too much. Usually the training periods weren't too effective.

It rocked on a day or two later. One evening, just before sundown, Sergeant White came in and had a first lieutenant with him, and the lieutenant told him to call attention. He commenced to do. (Attenhut!) Of course, most everyone slowly stood up, not standing at attention, but at least stood. Boy, he opened up and we thought he was the toughest and bravest man on earth to hear him talk. Everyone who had been in combat knew this would not last long. But we stayed there until November 19, then moved up to the front to cross the Meurthe River.

I would like to reflect back. While we were in this bivouac area in these pyramidal tents — every night a German airplane would come over. It was an intelligence plane and he was called "Bed Check Charlie." That was my first lesson because the older guys would tell us new ones, "Now you listen to the sound of the motor and you will be able to distinguish the German planes from the allied planes." Sure enough, before a week was over, the plane came over every night about the same time, and we got to where we could tell by the drone of the motor it was "Bed Check Charlie."

While I did not participate in any of the actual training, I hung around the company area all day and had chow and shaved. I didn't have too much to shave. We got replacements in, and I was placed in the first squad under Sergeant Breecy, who came back from the hospital. He was my squad leader and a very nice guy from Virginia. Another sergeant, named Forecrow from Texas, also came back with Breecy. I don't think we had but two squads, but maybe we had three. I don't seem to recall who the other squad leader was. We organized I recall I was the first scout, Tort was the second scout, and Breecy was the squad leader. We began to assemble our platoon. The first scout would lead the crossing, followed by the second scout, then by the rest of the platoon. I would need to go on out in the field. The second scout would be somewhere between me and the platoon and the rest of the company. We were led to believe that we were going to have some real opposition. We were also told that once we got across the river, to fix bayonets and to dig in. We went up near the river on the 19th and at 1:00 a.m. on the 20th of November, 1944, we were already across it.

In fact, we had ridden up to the Meurthe River, or in its vicinity. I don't know how far. We walked a good distance because the trucks couldn't get as close because of the enemy. The engineers had a pontoon bridge for us to cross, and as we neared the bridge, we saw these reflector lights on the bridge, which were reflecting back our way to show each side of it. It was a very small bridge. It didn't seem to be over three or four feet in width. However, it did go across the Meurthe River. It was dark and we couldn't see. You could hear the water running. It was a mountain stream and the water was cold and swift. I don't know what happened to us, but whoever was in charge, I assume it was an engineer, told us to close up tighter. We were stomach to back, that's the way we crossed. The weight of the main body got out on the pontoon bridge, and it sank down into the water over our knees. Consequently, water went down in our boots, and it was a number of days before I was able to get my feet warm. In fact, the current was so strong it knocked some of the guys off the bridge. This old man, Private Lowe in his late 30's, was swept off the bridge and drowned in the river. The younger fellas could take combat in this type of situation much better than the older ones. After crossing the river we did as instructed: we dug in, fixed our bayonets and waited. There was going to be a large artillery bombardment on the Germans. Just before daylight, they had all kinds of artillery zeroed in on the German positions, or what they thought were the German positions. They had ack-ack guns brought up near the river, and they were shooting. This made the Fourth of July or New Year's celebrations put on by our civic organizations look like a firecracker. It was magnificent, awesome and frightening. We could see tracer bullets line the sky. You knew for every tracer bullet, there must have been a dozen or more real bullets in the air. They had tanks, mortars, artillery, both small and great, firing. That was the most terrific bombardment I have ever seen, and one of the most awesome I ever witnessed in my life. I did witness a number of them later on, but I believe because this being the first one was most awesome. I don't recall how long this vast shelling went on, anywhere up to at least 45 minutes, then our guns suddenly went silent. No sooner had they become quiet, than the Germans suddenly opened up with a bombardment of their own, equal to the one our forces had performed. The thing that saved me from this bombardment, or from the exploding shells, was that the shells went over me. They felt like they were going to cut my head off — being so close to the ground. Nevertheless, I was at least a 100 or 200 yards ahead of the main forces. Consequently, I did not get shelled. I didn't know how many people were getting hit or anything.

I soon learned my squad leader, Sergeant Breecy, was hit by an 88 at very close range and it blew one of his legs off. Sergeant White told me he looked at Breecy and asked him, "Breecy, are you hurt?" Breecy replied, "White, I got it made." He was holding the stub of his leg in his hand, shaking it, and saying, "I got it made." No sooner had he said that, than he fell over dead. Sergeant Forecrow was killed immediately. As a result of that crossing, we lost 40 to 50 percent of our men.

Then they yelled for me to move out as soon as the German artillery let up. I started out slowly and was going very cautiously because I wanted them to catch up with me. I didn't want to get too far ahead. I heard a yelling noise. It seems the 3rd Battalion was behind us and they literally ran across those bridges because the Germans had not only shelled the side we were on, they had shelled the side we had just come from, and that's why they were waiting back there in reserve. They literally came at a right angle. I don't know which way they were going as far as directions were concerned. We took the Germans by surprise, because they hadn't taken the sign up off this mine field, but there wasn't any way we could see this at night: the sign saying "Minen," which meant, "This is a mine field." There's a picture in one of the history books, either in the Division Book or the 7th Regiment Book that shows this, but, nevertheless, the 3rd Battalion came at an angle and they were running in front of us, or ran in front of me. All of a sudden I saw the two lead men — I heard an explosion and saw these two men from the 3rd Battalion lifted up horizontally four, five feet high off the ground and there was a big blast and a loud explosion and they fell flat on the ground. When I saw this, I knew something was amiss.

It occurred to me that I was already in the mine field and I stopped dead still. I froze — afraid to move. I had been told in basic training about mine fields, but they had never made it exactly clear that the Germans had them, booby trapped like this situation. They would attach wires to the trigger mechanism on these mines and when you put your foot forward, the forward thrust would pull the wire tied to the trigger setting it off. If you stepped on it, the mine would explode. You were trapped two ways in this situation. If you didn't trip it, then you stepped on it.

A boy, Albert from Indiana, whom I had made friends with back where we had training, came up with Sergeant White and Lieutenant Sauer. Albert said, "Craft, we are in a mine field. What you have to do now is watch those wires and don't trip them. You watch where I step, raise your feet up high. Don't thrust them forward, and step in my footsteps." Well, I followed Albert exactly through the mine field. Sauer was going to trust White, but White wasn't being quite as generous with the lieutenant as Albert was with me. So Sauer decided he would follow me, taking each step I took, and we got to the embankment. As far as I know, the rest of the ones, who were not hurt at the river, got through this mine field. We came to some concertina wire on a little ridge or embankment. I helped cut the wire but we ran on to some more, which was wider. We had a bandilow torpedo. It was a long tube, and had an explosive in it. You inserted it through the wire, lit the fuse and it would blow a hole large enough allowing us to pass through. This slowed us down for a few minutes; however, we continued the attack through this open field and got on top of a hill — going down the hill was a mound of dirt.

As first scout, I was leading. A German stepped out of a pillbox wanting to surrender, but only to an officier (officer), as he called it. I told him to put his hands up. Albert saw a smoke stack coming out of the mound of dirt which covered and camouflaged the top of the pillbox, and shot down the pipe. A medic came running out, scared to death, with both hands reaching for the sky. The officer was a captain. He had to be taken back and released to the people in charge of prisoners. I volunteered, and Sergeant White said, "Fine." I got them back a short distance and the German officer didn't want to hold his hands up. I had a little conversation with him and threw up my gun to shoot him. A battalion headquarters officer came up and witnessed this incident. He said to me, "Soldier, if he doesn't do what you tell him, shoot the son-of-a-bitch." I threw up my gun to shoot, and the German officer's hands flew to the sky. The lieutenant laughed saying, "Good work, soldier, I'll take over." Later, I learned he directed the shelling on us at the Meurthe River.

The day we jumped off in this river crossing attack at Sergeant White's suggestion, I went to the aid station and had my right sore thumb inspected by the doctor who was an officer. He put merthiolate on it and started to bandage it. During this process, I mentioned to him my thumb was sore. It was the one I used to load my M-1 rifle, and because of the soreness and the bandage, it would be impossible to load my rifle and be an effective soldier. He grunted it would not hinder me and said to report for duty, knowing he was wrong. The soldier that he examined before me was goldbricking and was sent back to the hospital. I knew this fellow from basic training and he was a yellow coward. That's the justice of the Army. It seems your life hinges on an officer's whim, whether doctor, chaplain or any other son of a bitch who wore a bar on his shoulder. Knowing this, I did not protest but went on back and led our battalion as first scout.

Hurlache, France, at 1635 was our objective. The first shooting fight engaging the Krauts, my rifle clip was emptied and had to be reloaded. In the heat of the battle, I reached and took a new clip of ammunition and without thinking, loaded my rifle. As I suspected, when I released the spring, the bolt flew forward catching the bandage and pulling it off. My thumb nail was sticking straight up bleeding. Reaching down with my left hand I jerked the nail completely off and, although it was sore and hurting, I could at least load my rifle and kill Krauts. All this time I was cursing the stupid officer, who called himself a doctor. The thumb was sore and hurt when I used it, but in the heat of combat, it did not bother me, as the many occasions I had to shoot the Krauts, the thumb was forgotten. However, the nail did not heal properly and to this day, 40 years later, my right thumb nail is rough and somewhat difficult to trim or clip, because it is unusually hard and brittle.

We proceeded forward all day long and had to clear a wooded area on a hill. We got in the wooded area and a group of our P-51 fighter planes began to strafe this area. It was an awesome and terrible feeling. We were frightened out of our wits. Finally, the Company Commander got the battalion on radio, who got word to the pilots that they were strafing their own troops. After a long period of time they quit, but it was a terrible experience. We cleared this area and proceeded toward Hurlache, France, our objective, as I have previously stated. We captured the town after sporadic fighting all day long and into the night.

We took over a house and made it platoon CP. In the infantry, CP is an abbreviation for command post. You had Company Command Post and each platoon command post, and CP was shorter to say. Anyway, we got set up in the house. It was a small house. Part of the platoon was sent further out to guard, to pull guard duty that night. But I was allowed to stay there at the house, probably on orders from Sauer, because he seemed to attach himself to me. Consequently, I was able to stay in the house part of the night, at least four hours and then go out and pull four hours guard duty. It was raining and bitter cold. The Germans were trying to infiltrate our positions. They knew where we were. We never knew exactly where they were. We expected them to be any place. There was shouting and shooting going on all night long, which was typical throughout my period in combat. You never had much sleep or rest. It was always harassment. Even when you pulled up some place you could hear the fighting and you had that fear of "Well, when are we going to get into the fighting?" but once you got into the battle, fears seemed to leave you.

The next morning I was on guard duty at the break of day and I will never forget this incident. It was very amusing, and all of us got a big laugh out of it.

The Germans used horses some in their combat operations and that came as a surprise to me. I thought they were a modern mechanical army, but at times they used horses to pull artillery and other things. Apparently, two Germans had hidden out during the night. Early the next morning they found a horse, hitched it to a two-wheel wagon and made a break for it. With the horse running at full speed, they got away amid heavy fire. I never did hear to the contrary, but we all got a big kick out of it, saying, "We'll get them later on." I then learned that my friend, Johnny Clayton, had been wounded on the river crossing.

Shortly after that we proceeded into the attack walking, but not meeting much opposition. My socks and feet were still wet from the river crossing two days earlier. We walked all day hunting the Krauts. This would have been November 21, 1944. We came to a huge forest that night, dug in, taking shifts on guard. As we were marching into the attack, we could hear church bells ringing in French villages. We were not marching on the road, but off the road at the edge of the forest which concealed our presence. It was heavy and difficult walking in mountainous country. I had heard a war had never been fought through these mountains before.

That didn't make sense to me because in one breath I heard there had never been a battle fought in the Voseges Mountains before, and then finding these trenches, it was conflicting. Apparently, this information was untrue because I later discovered in while reading an article about Harry Truman, that during World War I he had fought in this same area. Nevertheless, we went on and had a few skirmishes. We must have been in regimental reserve (our battalion) and that night we came to a forest and bedded down right on the edge of it in foxholes. The next morning some trucks came up and we all loaded on them and drove for some time; I don't know how long. Then they put us out, and we began walking again. This was when we ran across the dugouts from what they said was the old French Maginot Line. Shortly after we got there, we explored those a little bit. We looked at them and they were in complete ruins. We approached the town on the 22nd. We were going down a street and had not run into much resistance. One of our tanks moving through into Able Company's area, made the curve at the intersection, turned left and straightened out, hitting a mine which knocked his track off, slowing us down.

Some of the higher-ups decided we should advance through a big field out to our front, and sloping up into a wooded area. There was another smaller meadow, and there was a smaller wooded area before you got to the small meadow. Upon reaching the small wooded area, Sergeant White ordered the scouts to cross this meadow and go over and check out the forest ahead of the main force. That included scouts of the first and second squads of the 1st Platoon of Charlie Company. By this time a replacement named Younger, from Arkansas was first scout, with me being second scout of the first squad.

A small fellow named Dossi, from Brooklyn, New York, was the first scout, with a big fellow who wore a mustache named Medger and the second scout of the second squad. Younger went first, the first squad being on the right and the second squad on the left. We were in a staggered formation. Dossi was slightly behind Younger, and I was slightly behind Younger and Dossi. Medger was behind us all. As soon as all four of us were well into the meadow, a German ack-ack gun was shooting exploding shells, they usually shot at airplanes. They exploded when they hit a target. He cut down on

Younger, killing him instantly. The German gunner used good strategy, because he prevented Younger from getting into the woods. He swung down on Medger and hit him. It didn't kill him instantly; however, he died of wounds later on.

The German swung his gun from Medger back to Dossi, who was then the advancing man and by the time he started shooting at Dossi, he had buried himself into a pile of cow manure the Frenchman stacked in their field for fertilizer purposes in the spring. In my position, there was nothing to get behind or under. I fell face down on the ground. He shot at Dossi and you could see the cow manure splatter, but old Dossi didn't get a scratch. Thinking he got Dossi, he shot at me. The first time he shot, the bullets hit the ground about six inches from my head, kicking up the dirt. Then the gunner, to make sure, shot at me again. He missed me another six inches from my feet. By that time, the ack-ack gun stopped shooting, and Sergeant White yelled for us to come back. I wouldn't stand up because I didn't know what was going on and slid backwards. My shirt was pulled out of my trousers and I was disorganized, disoriented and, frankly, scared to death. Moments later, old Dossi came back and he was literally covered with cow manure and you know the odor of that! We shied away from him for several days. Later on, I found out this little guy who had the crabs at Fort Meade, Maryland, named Anders, was the one that sneaked up on the German shooting the ack-ack gun at us. He shot him in the head with a bazooka; that's what stopped the ack-ack gun and saved our lives.

When we got back into the little wooded strip, there were several colonels in that vicinity and one of them looked at me. I was dirty, frightened and he looked at Dossi. He says, "What's the matter with you boys? There's nothing going on." He was walking calmly around as if nothing had ever happened. We told him, "If you had been where we were you wouldn't be walking around so cocky either, because he almost got us. He got two out of four." We didn't want to make an issue out of it, but he did have an advantage. He had a radio and knew what was going on. We licked our wounds a short time and the higher brass decided for us to cross the meadow again. I got a promotion back to first scout and Albert replaced me as second scout. After crossing this meadow, we headed into the forest padded with pine or some type of evergreen needles that had fallen off the trees.

I found a trail and everyone fell in behind me. We were staggered in formation to prevent a machine gun from getting all of us at one time. We had traveled a short distance and the trail indicated we were going up hill. I was being very careful and cautious. As I walked along I noticed a machine gun traversing its barrel back and forth. I immediately jumped to my left, off the trail, and observed the machine gun slowly being withdrawn back over the crest and disappear. Albert laughed and asked, "What's wrong, Craft, are you getting gun shy? There's nothing up there." I'll admit being shy, but I clearly saw this happen and after reflecting on this incident many times, I know the Lord intervened and spared my life again. We walked and walked and finally cleared the forest. We spent the night of November 22, 1944, at the edge of the forest again, pulling four hours on and off guard, and the next morning we loaded on trucks again.

Shortly before getting to Saales, the first Alsace town liberated, we unloaded from the trucks, not knowing our location or destination. We were on our way to Saales to help the 3rd Battalion. They had barrelled right on through the German defense and captured Saales, catching the Germans by surprise. For the most part they had captured the town, but there was still a lot of shooting going on. On some of the streets we had to cross, the Germans had machine guns zeroed in on the intersections. We would stop at the street corner and wait for the machine gun to stop firing, then we'd dart across. As each GI darted across the street, the enemy machine gun would open up. That's the way the 1st Battalion managed to get through Saales. We went on through the town, not knowing what our objective was. The enlisted men didn't, but as it turned out, we were on our way to a night of misery and hell.

CHAPTER 10
THE BATTLE OF BOURG-BRUCHE THANKSGIVING, 1944

Able Company was leading the way, with Charlie following them and B Company was in the reserve. We were going down a road, and it was dark. My boots were squashing because water was still in them. I hadn't had time to change socks or pull off my boots. It had been raining on and off all day. Since the 19th, we had gotten very little sleep. (This was the 23rd)! We were going night and day. I was walking along, and I would drop off to sleep walking.

Able Company ran into some opposition up ahead of us and were sending out patrols testing the German defense. To our right flank, we saw Germans on a hill, silhouetted in the moonlight, and started shooting and killed them. My primary job was to keep contact with A Company. Old Mal Atney, the arrogant first lieutenant, acting company commander, came up to make sure that we still had contact with A Company and he asked, Sergeant White if we were maintaining contact.

Sergeant White told him, "Yeah, Craft's keeping in contact with them."

I said, "There they are! I'm not letting them out of my sight."

He said, "Soldier, if you lose contact with A Company, I'm going to break every damn bone in your body." I didn't respond; I wanted to shoot him, but nevertheless, Able Company broke through the roadblock and we followed them into the town of Bourg—Bruche. I do not know how far this roadblock was from town, but I remember we kept going straight at an intersection and I didn't know what was going on.

For some reason, there was confusion and Battalion Commander Collen and his staff were drinking heavy and said we had to turn to the right. Able Company came back and got on the road to Bourg-Bruche. Able Company was ahead of us on the road. As soon as we got near to the entrance of the town, a German machine gun opened fire on us. The Krauts had an elaborate defense set up — it wasn't fully manned at all times, but if they had had greater numbers in manpower, I don't see how we would have ever broken their defense. When this machine gun opened up, I remember the instructions pointed out by the field training sergeant in basic training: Take cover and then shoot. Out of the corner of my eye, I saw a German foxhole. It was different from the ones we dug. It was a one man foxhole, where you were able to stand up and shoot a rifle, then duck down into the hole. I made a leap four or five feet to my right, and I struck this foxhole dead center. When I landed, I plunged down and it was half full of water. I was in water from about my hips down and my feet were already wet. I was wet, tired and cold.

The machine gun was silenced with the help of a tank, who performed beautifully, and we went on into town following Able Company, who was taking prisoners. Charlie Company went through them. There was so much confusion, it being dark, we had the Germans completely disorganized. They were running everywhere, and we were shooting at them and at one another. One of our medics was walking along the street, and he came face to face with a Kraut.

The Jerry had a burp gun and shot Doc point blank, only knocking his belt buckle off. Medics didn't carry weapons. Poor Doc was unable to defend himself, but through a miracle, he escaped death. Those of us, who were in a group, 1st Platoon leading, followed by the 2nd Platoon, then the 3rd Platoon, decided it was best to secure a house where we could better defend ourselves. We turned up the street to the right and I yelled out, "Here's a house," and ran down to the entrance. I had my hand on the doorknob and I was suddenly pushed from behind and a guy said, "Soldier, I'm Lieutenant Broate, an officer of the United States Army, and this is my house." I was a little bit taken aback, and he opened the door. When he did, a German potato masher hit him in the face. This is an example of how the officers tried to pull rank and get more favorable positions, but you see, God had his hand in this thing. If I had opened the door, I would have gotten the potato masher.

By that time, Sergeant White had gotten back there. I don't know what happened to the brave Lieutenant Willie Sauer. We got in this house by capturing one German. It was never known whether he was the one who threw the grenade or not, but my personal belief was he fled up the stairs and jumped out the back window. There were German bunks in this house, apparently they were billeted there. We searched upstairs and couldn't find any more Krauts. We couldn't have light. All of a sudden, the Germans counter-attacked, shooting rifles, grenades and bazookas. We fought them all through the night.

The 3rd Platoon had gone into a house further up and across the street, four or five houses down, and we could hear them fighting and we could hear Sergeant Stern. He could speak German. He was yelling out to them in German. They were yelling out to us in German to surrender and we wouldn't do it. It was really difficult. They had so demoralized us, that it was really difficult for us to get someone to go protect and guard the front door. We did survive that night, and Stern's platoon did by the hardest. There were remnants of the 1st and 2nd Platoon in this house and the 3rd Platoon was up the street. We had fought the Germans all night long and when it seemed like they were getting the best of us, we began to call for our tanks, as there was one tank beside our building. As usual, the tankers were too yellow to come to our aid, as they could have poked their nose around the corner and shot the Germans up, but it took an order from the battalion commander to get them to move. As we would yell, "Tanks, tanks," the Germans, not understanding what we meant, were mimicking us by yelling "tanks, tanks." They had the advantage that night, but our revenge was sweet the next day.

We got up the next morning — there was a wall out front, we hadn't seen the night before. Getting behind the wall, four or five feet high, old Atney came up and said, "We have to clear those houses out and there are a lot of them." I don't know how many there were. He said, "1st Platoon will take the lead. Sergeant White, get your scouts out."

White yelled out, "First scout, 1st Platoon" and looked over at me. I was sitting down, leaning against the wall and White says, "Well, I can't send you first, Craft. I'll lead and you follow me." White led the way! We cleared a house or two and didn't find anything. The third house was a tavern. White busted the door open and went in. He was ahead of me and I went on through, and I knew he had veered off to the right. As I was coming into the doorway, there was a full length mirror on the wall, and I saw myself in the mirror. I thought it was a German, never having seen myself in combat attire. I threw up my gun to shoot and almost pulled the trigger; then I realized what it was and felt very foolish. White was down to the right.

This building was built in a peculiar shape. We heard a dog barking and couldn't figure out where the sound was coming from. It sounded like he was beneath us. We looked for stairways, but couldn't find any stairs. In the middle of a long room, we saw a small rug. It looked a little suspicious. We moved the rug, finding a trap door. We opened this trapdoor, and a little white dog came sprinting out. It was a very small dog with long white hair. I don't know what breed he was, but you could hold him in your hand. We heard women crying, and two old ladies came up the stairs and when they found out that we were Americans, they were very happy. They hugged us and began to jabber in French.

They gave us what they could in the way of food and made us welcome, told us to build a fire and make ourselves comfortable. They also warned us that the Germans had left at daybreak and were up in the field near the wooded areas across the railroad tracks and were preparing to counterattack. It was a railroad bridge built up over the streets.

We went up on the third floor and the company commander was notified. He came up and we told him of our conversation with the French women. He got on his radio and called back for artillery. In the meantime, he had taken his field glasses and could see the activity going on out there. With his field glasses, he could pick out an anti—tank gun, a tank and he could see that enemy soldiers had dug into the field in their foxholes. He ordered artillery.

In the meantime, we passed the word back for everybody to be on the alert, that the Germans were entrenched and getting ready to counter—

attack. He ordered the first shot. It was about 100 yards over the target. He told them to cut it down 200 yards and the artillery fired another smoke shell and it was short. He told them to increase the last shot by 100 yards and to fire for effect. That's all the artillery needed! Boy, did they perform a beautiful job! They put in a heavy barrage of artillery and the Germans began coming out of the foxholes.

Everyone had a field day in picking the Germans off as they came out of the foxholes. It felt real good shooting those Krauts; it felt like killing dirty flea-infested rats. I was told back then there was a battalion of them; there weren't many of them that were captured, most of them were killed. Perhaps a few of the dirty rats got away. Anyway, our 1st Sergeant Wicks looked out across the field and saw two German soldiers leading six GI prisoners in single file across the field toward the wooded area, about 500 yards away. He picked up his rifle, using good strategy by shooting the Kraut at the rear, then shot and killed the German who was leading.

Immediately, the medics ran toward our lines. It was our medics they had captured! When we broke through the roadblock, the medics were following us at a good distance and before they got to the roadblock, the Germans had re-established it, hoping to trap us. Instead, they captured our medics. That was a happy occasion to get our medics back. We fought all day long and when noon time came — everybody was getting hungry — word got around that rations had been brought up, and for us to send one man to get them at a certain place. I was told where they were; every platoon was sending someone for rations. I ran into several fellows, who were going back for the rations for their various platoons, and a German machine gunner had found out that was the place where the rations were, and he was shooting from pretty long distance. Every time, somebody would go in or out the door, he'd shoot. There was a GI ahead of me. He went first and opened the door and went on in. Immediately, after he went in, the door closing behind him, the Germans shot several bursts from the machine gun. I did the same thing, running real fast, I pulled the door open and went on in. Behind me, bullets came through the door. There were one or two other guys behind me, who did the same thing. We all got in safe and received our rations. The GI, who was dishing out the rations said, "Don't go back through that front door. He'll get you for sure. Go out the back door and down a few houses and cut across." That was a very difficult thing to do, because there were so many obstacles in doing this. We were totally unfamiliar with the town, having just gotten there the night before. There were walls and things you had to go over and you didn't know what was on the other side. We got our chow bags, made our way back to the platoon and shared the rations with everyone. The rations tasted real good, as we had not eaten in 24 hours.

It was late afternoon and one of their machine guns kept firing and harassing us. It had to be stopped and the 1st Platoon of Charlie Company was selected to do the job. Lieutenant Sauer had gotten back into the picture somewhere. I don't know where he came from, but he was probably back there where it was safe, you can bet your boots on that. He called us all together in a huddle and said, "It has become our objective to go up and knock this machine gun out." He looked at me and said, "Craft, you are the first scout. You are going to go right behind the tank. Everybody else will be lined up behind you." Colonel Collen was standing over to my left front a little way from us and he heard this conversation.

He came over to our group and said, "Lieutenant, like hell, you are going behind the tank. You are going in front of it. The tank's more important to us than you are or any of your men." The lieutenant turned white as a sheet, and I know I did, too, because I didn't want to face the machine gun, especially going up hill. Lieutenant Sauer recovered his composure and said, "All right, Craft, we will be ahead of and all around the tank, but you'll be leading the way."

We were organized into the formation, ready to go after the machine gun. We heard a commotion and looked to our left. I know this (the Lord intervened again) because we saw a battalion of GIs and somebody said they were veering up to their right, up the road, where the machine gun was firing. Somebody said, "That's the 3rd Battalion. They are going through us."

Collen came over and said, "Never mind, boys. We don't have to take this machine gun. That's the 3rd Battalion's objective."

Now I was thankful and relieved. I spoke to myself and said, "Thank you, Lord." Ironically, that machine gun never fired again. I don't know what happened to it. I suppose they saw the battalion of men coming their way. They knew they couldn't hold out, so they either surrendered or left. I did not bother to find out.

As stated before, this town was called Bourg—Bruche and this happened on Thursday, November 23, 1944. For this bitter fight, I have skipped many details, but it was one of the most frightening times of my life. I had many scary times. Our battalion, in taking Nayemont and Bourg-Bruche, received the Presidential Unit Citation, which was a coveted award, because that particular medal wasn't given out freely. We stayed in the town that night and the next day, and I didn't do anything but rest. Johnny Clayton went up to look at the dead Germans and he came back and looked me up and said, "Craft, have you been up there to see those dead Germans?"

I said, "No."

He said, "I have. I've never seen as many dead people in all my life. There are so many, you can hardly walk without stepping on them."

I told him I had no desire to go up there and see the Krauts, as long as they were dead, that was fine with me. Johnny Clayton filled me in on how he had gotten hit at the Meurthe River Crossing, but they kept him at a field hospital a couple of days and then sent him back to the front. He caught up with us, after we captured Bourg-Bruche. I related to him about the events and his platoon leader, Lieutenant Broate, and he could hardly believe it. Johnny Clayton was one of my best friends, and we always got together and talked whenever possible.

CHAPTER 11
ON TO STRASBOURG - THE CHAMPAGNE CITY OF EUROPE

Sometime during the night, we were loaded onto trucks and we went a great distance. We didn't know what was going on. We were put out into a town, which was Strasbourg. It was called "The Champagne City of Europe." It was a resort city on the Rhine, where champagne was made and entertainment for people from all over the world. There was a sports center right on the Rhine River. The French 2nd Army had broken through and had captured most of Strasbourg. This put us on the Rhine River, and the 7th Army was 80 miles ahead of all the other allies, including Patton's 3rd Army. The enemy had taken its toll on all of our units, as we were about one third of the normal number of men. Dossi was ahead of me, and we were marching up to this big mansion into a huge courtyard. This was what they called Alsace-Lorraine, the area where the French and the Germans had fought for centuries over ownership. Strasbourg was the capital city of the Alsace-Lorriane Area.

In World War I the French got it back, and the Germans had it when they over ran it in World War II, so we had liberated it from the Germans. We found out that these people were mixed. They were French and German.

There was a great, big civilian. I don't know how old he was. He was in a gateway into either a town or one of the mansions. He was drinking Schnapps, which was a German liquor. He was happy because we had liberated them. He held out his hand with a bottle and said, "Schnapps" and ole Dossi was a very small man. I was five feet and seven inches tall and he was at least two, maybe three inches shorter than I, although he was older. Dossi leaped up and grabbed the bottle out of the man's hand and put it to his lips, and took a long swig and passed it back to me. I took a long swig and passed it back to the next man, and by the time it got to the end of the line, the poor fellow didn't have any left.

We stayed in some buildings that night. The next day, we cleared out an area of buildings not meeting much resistance. All of the units of the 3rd Division had pushed up to a canal, where there was a large pocket of the enemy on our side of the Rhine. They had good defensive positions and their artillery and mortars constantly harassed us from the pocket and from across the Rhine. This pocket of the enemy was called the Kehl Bridgehead. We had captured numerous warehouses, which stored all types of supplies, which included uniforms, underwear, food of all kinds and all sorts of military hardware and ammunition. In going through the food warehouse, I saw some canned sardines. Back home in Smith County, Mississippi, this was one of my favorite fish foods. I picked up three or four cans and ate them, though they were not prepared the same way as I was accustomed. When night came, Albert and I were assigned to an outpost on the canal. The Germans knew we were there, and they shelled us unmercifully all night long. We had a phone and reported into the platoon command post. Along about 3:00 AM, I developed an upset stomach and had to have a bowel movement. Every time I attempted to get out of the foxhole, the Germans would start shelling, and the shells were exploding so close that I didn't have time to let my trousers down and let mother nature act. I jumped back in the foxhole with Albert, trying to hold my bowels in check, but the shells kept falling so nature had its way and my loose bowels moved into my clothes. What a dirty smell! I felt miserable. I suffered for a while, then jumped out of the foxhole in spite of the shelling and removed my clothes, using the dry part of my underwear to clean myself, then discarded the underwear and put my OD's back on. I jumped back in the foxhole and called the platoon command post and talked to Sergeant White, telling him that I had eaten the German sardines and developed a bad case of the GI's. I had crapped in my pants and had to throw away my underwear. Boy, did he laugh! Much to my discomfort, he agreed to contact Alfred, the supply sergeant and obtain some underwear for me.

Shortly before daybreak, the remainder of Charlie Company came down, and we were told that we were going to cross the canal on a railroad bridge and the 1st Platoon was to lead the attack. As first scout, I was to lead. On two previous occasions, two other infantry companies had tried to cross, but they had to retreat because of the heavy resistance put up by the Krauts, as they were strongly fortified. The previous night, Johnny Clayton, my buddy went over the bridge and shot the Germans up, but because of heavy resistance had to retreat after killing several Germans. This four man patrol received a Silver Star each.

Sergeant White and myself got on the bridge, one on each side. I was leading this time and we both made a running charge, followed by Albert. The Germans opened up with machine guns, mortars and their riflemen were shooting, but they couldn't stop us. Sergeant White and I got across the bridge and we heard some Germans talking. I hollered for them to come out, but they wouldn't budge. Sergeant White told me to throw a chemical grenade, which I did, and that really brought them out. We got five or six prisoners. That seemed to demoralize the Germans and within 10 minutes, we had about 37 prisoners. We pushed on! Being first scout, I had to lead the way. We ran into a little opposition and there was heavy firing down near the apartment buildings. The 2nd Battalion had the job of clearing that out.

We came to a playground or some sort of stadium. We got out into the middle of the stadium and it had open bleachers on one side, similar to the ones that are used today, here in Memphis, Tennessee, for the elementary and high schools. We ran across this playground/field under heavy enemy machine gun fire. The only cover we had was the bleachers and we were losing some men under maddening machine gun fire. We got under the bleachers for cover. The Germans couldn't see us. They had us pinned down.

Eventually, we worked ourselves out of this and got the Germans, and by that time, it was getting late in the evening. The company commander, old Atney, said, we had to contact the 3rd Battalion. They wanted a two man patrol to go contact the 3rd Battalion. White selected me and Sergeant Silks to go on this patrol. They oriented us on where we should go and we went. This was my second contact patrol. My first one was a disaster, because of the loss of Willard Clark, and I was fearful. Silks didn't seem to mind. Artillery was bursting all around us and we could hear the machine guns rattling. We made contact with the 3rd Battalion, secured the needed information, went back and reported to Atney. We had the 1st Platoon back under the command of brave Lieutenant Willie Sauer. Our objective was to go clear some wooded areas and I don't know what possessed Sauer, I guess he had a lot of confidence in me, because he did not want to go anywhere unless I was in front of him. I went up every trail, scouted it out for safety, then the son-of-a-bitch would follow, when I reported it was clear. I got so tired that night, it seemed as if we walked all night long. We got this big pocket cleared out. Then they pulled us back into a big factory building. An officer from Battalion Headquarters received a high medal for Sergeant White's and my charge across the bridge. We were still in Strasbourg. It was a dangerous situation. The people spoke German and French.

Incidentally, the day we got there, the Strasbourg bank had not closed. It was still open and two GIs robbed it. I heard later our friend Anders from Fort Meade, Maryland, was one of them, and he and his buddy got away with several million franks. They stayed in Strasbourg and shacked up until the end of the war. Whether this was true, I don't know, but that's what I heard from my friend, Clayton.

We were pulled back into this big factory building and while we were quite crowded, we did have the warmth of the building. One of Charlie Company's duties was to guard a huge bridge. It was comparable to the big viaduct on Jackson Avenue, here in Memphis, perhaps longer. Apparently, it was very important, because they were afraid the Germans would blow it up, as some of the Gèrmans had changed to civilian clothes. They were armed and trained to blow up bridges and spy. Several were captured! Albert and I were guard buddies that night. It was so cold and we were out with no protection from the bitter, wintry wind. Albert started prowling around. He found a dead German, looted him and found salami, bread and a bottle of Apricot Brandy. He brought it back and we took several slugs out of it, and ate the food when we got off guard duty, about 2:00 a.m. in the morning. We went back to this factory and some of the guys were coming in. We gave them a drink, and took a couple more drinks ourselves. That was the best drink I ever had in my life. I suppose it was because my body was so cold. It was enough to warm me up, and I went to sleep.

Finally, the city was cleared of Germans. We were moved into enemy barracks and had sheets, blankets and hot chow. Our duties now were to guard the Rhine. We went up and stayed two days and two nights in bunkers taking our rations. Instead of keeping us by platoons, if there were any extras, they put us with D Company, the weapons platoon of our battalion. I was put with D Company, and didn't know any of those guys, and had to pull the most dangerous guard post. I didn't get my share of the chow, because they cheated me out of it. I was pretty well disgusted when I got back to the barracks, but at the end of the week the Company had gotten some cognac. They got two bottles for each GI, and we weren't having to pull guard any more. Just had to pull this watch for a week on the Rhine. Towards the end of the week we had a party, took our liquor to our barracks and sat down and began to drink and raise cain. I was so disgusted by this time I was getting pretty well hardened. I drank too much cognac.

In the barracks where we were, the Germans had a delivery place for the kitchen that we used. Our big trucks coming in and out had gotten it so mushy that you'd bog down to your knees. Someone mentioned the fact that they had a guitar over in the mess hall and we were going to get one of the cooks to play for us. Rather than go the long way around, Albert and I were about halfway drunk. He put his boots on, laced up and tied, but I didn't lace mine up, and I had the wrong boots. I got the boots of a little Italian fellow, whose name I have forgotten. He was a quiet fellow and every time an artillery shell came over, whether close or not, he'd duck and fall to the ground. You could see the fear in his eyes. When we went for the guitar through the mud, my boots weren't laced up and they got stuck in the mud. I pulled my feet out of them and left the boots there. I went back without my boots, guitar or player. Sergeant White said, "Let the boots stay out there." We drank more cognac, raised cain and finally went to bed. During the night I got sick and vomited on the little Italian's bed and mine, too. The next morning, he was giving me heck about messing up his bed, but I was so sick I didn't pay any attention to him. Everyone was getting dressed and putting on their boots. He couldn't find his and had a pair in his hands that did not fit.

I said, "Yeah, those are mine."

He said, "Where's mine?"

"I guess I lost them in that mud last night."

He became very angry; he went out in the mud and retrieved his boots.

When he came back, he was really cursing me out. I apologized, but he kept on and would not shut up. I called his hand and told him I'd whip his ass if he didn't leave me alone. I was tired of fooling with him. He left me alone, cleaned his boots, and I've forgotten what happened to him.

One day we were just loafing around not doing anything much, because it only took a limited number of us to pull guard, and they stretched it out as far as they could. On this particular day, we were all whiling away time and had gotten some German Limburger cheese. This same little Italian went to sleep and had his mouth opened. We were sitting on his bunk. I looked around and saw the open mouth. I put some Limburger cheese in it. That's horrible stuff! He chewed it, swallowed it, and it didn't even wake him up! We all got a big bang out of that, because we were pulling pranks and that kind of stuff to shift our nervousness.

While in Strasbourg, I went looking for a clock and found a nice one that was beautiful and chimed. However, the Kraut artillery started coming in, and I dropped it, breaking it to shreds.

CHAPTER 12
THREE DAY PASS

Lo and behold, it came up that I had a three day pass, back to Bourbonne les Baines, the division rest camp. I rode in a truck a long time. We arrived at the division rest camp, where there was good entertainment, the 3rd Division Band and some very pretty girls. There was also a radio, and the Red Cross had a huge dayroom where we could write letters. This was the only service I got out of the Red Cross, a quiet facility to write letters back home. Also in the kitchen, dances were held every night for the GIs. I couldn't dance, but those civilians like to come in and dance with the soldiers, especially the waltzes.

Every night while we were there, we could hear Axis Sally shooting her propaganda and telling us various thing about the 4F'ers sleeping with our wives and making big money, while we were fighting a war we could not win. She'd call the 3rd Division names and tell us we ought to go home. We didn't mind this too much. We knew it was propaganda and it really did amuse us.

In the division rest camp, the Army had brought in some Spanish prostitutes, and any GI could go in and pay the fee and engage in sex. Before he was allowed to leave, however, he had to take a prophylaxis treatment under the supervision of a medical doctor.

Also in Bourbonne les Baines, there was a man who ran a beer joint or saloon. He had stayed over in France from the First World War and married. He was one of the first civilian men that I heard speak fluent English, although we did not talk much. He told White to never marry a French woman. He further stated that he was from east Tennessee, and Sergeant White knew his family.

While in camp I ran into Johnny Clayton. He was telling me about everyone of the boys who took basic with us. They had either been seriously wounded or killed and that was very depressing. I fully enjoyed my three days, because I had no combat. It was a long way from the lines. We kept ourselves busy, talking and playing cards, writing letters and listening to Axis Sally, watching the boys and girls dance. We listened to the radio and other things, too. We could go to concerts put on by the division band. They had singers with their good band, and they played popular songs. We had movies that were free. The chow was good, too. We enjoyed warm beds and would have liked to stay longer, but our three days were up, and we headed back to the front lines.

We got on some trucks and the drivers going toward the front lines were scared and liquored up. I don't know how or where we went, but it seemed as if they were exceeding the speed limit, almost bumper to bumper, without lights. That ride back took us one or two days and nights, but I was really glad to get back. They didn't take us back to Strasbourg. We had heard the Division, the same day we left, was alerted to go to the Colmar Pocket, and that's where they carried us. We stayed in a hayloft that night and that was the last night I spent in a house for three months.

CHAPTER 13
COLMAR POCKET CAMPAIGN
(December 21, 1944 - February 18, 1945)

We had a lucky break from the Meurthe River to Strasbourg located on the Rhine. The French 2nd Armoured Division captured most of the town leaving us the Kehl Bridgehead to complete. We completely surprised the Germans with good strategy, dogged determination and hard fighting. However, the 7th Infantry Regiment, which was my combat unit, were the first American troops to reach the Rhine River.

We completely captured the town by December 2, 1944. We thought we would have to cross the river at the point which led into the Black Forest and apparently it was heavily defended, as there were pill boxes lined up on the other side. Sergeant White, my platoon sergeant, was chosen to go with Colonel Collen and another officer in a jeep as a gunner with a .50 caliber machine gun. They crossed the bridge over the Cliner Rhine and returned without much action. White did get a little gun practice on a few Krauts, who quickly took cover. However, the other 36th Army Division, along with the French, had not been so fortunate as they had run into fierce opposition from the Krauts in an area called by several names, but eventually called the Colmar Pocket.

The enemy decided to hold onto Colmar and set up strong defensive positions in the Voseges Mountains to the west of the city. The Rhine plain in Alsace between the Voseges and the great river is cut by numerous rivers and streams and has an elaborate system of canals. The Krauts used these water barriers to protect this bridgehead from attack, either from the north or the south. The 1st French Army had tried and failed to penetrate the territory held by the enemy and did not gain a thing. The result was that the German lines surrounding Colmar became a virtual ring of steel, as the enemy implaced himself in the most strategic positions the mountain studded regions, rivers and canals afforded. The French and the 36th Divisions (American) were having difficulty and the 3rd Division was called upon to replace the 36th Division and at that time became attached to the French Army. Snow had already covered the ground with six or eight inches. It was discovered that nine enemy divisions were defending this area, and three of them opposed the American 36th, alone.

When we first got to the Colmar Pocket, the 3rd Division had to attack to get in better defensive positions. This dreadful fight for Colmar was overlooked due to German success in Von Rundstadt's offensive in the north involving Bastogne and Patton's 3rd Army. According to the older men in our outfit, the bitter fighting through the Voseges and Colmar Pocket was much worse than the well publicized Anzio Beachhead in which the 3rd Division fought.

There were SS troops, mountain troops and a group of officers from Officers Candidate School who were offered a commission if they went to Colmar and succeeded in holding the Colmar Pocket. The Germans did not want to leave this last parcel of French soil; neither did they want to give up the bridge across the Rhine, which was vital to their supply route and escape route, if they could not hold it. The deep snow and bitter cold hampered both sides, but it probably hurt us more, because we had to hunt them down in the cold, rarely seeing the inside of a house. They had houses, liquor and some of the more fanatical had drugs to help their nerves, while we lived and fought in the snowy winter without a blanket.

We were issued GI gloves, but you couldn't load the M-1 with your right hand, inadvertently losing it, and when the fight was over the right glove was missing. If you touched the metal on the rifle, your fingers would stick. All of these things, mixed with the Kraut determination to hold at all cost, made this type of fighting more unpleasant. This was a vicious enemy as our wounded were booby trapped. Doors on houses were booby trapped, and mines were laid, where they knew we would have to cross. Every place was marked for artillery, as they used it extensively and successfully.

The German 88 was most effective. I know ours was as good, if not better. They were very skillful in laying in wait and ambushing us. No doubt this was the bitterest, fiercest battle that went on in World War II, when most people thought it was over. Perhaps General Patch, Commander of the 7th Army, did not have the public relations people to report the 7th Army achievements or maybe he wanted to do the job in a quiet manner. I don't want to be misunderstood. I admired Patton for his foresight and wisdom in defeating the Germans, but his feats were accomplished on the plains and with armour.

This was getting along about December 21, 1944, and I was assigned to a foxhole with Albert. He had, by that time, become my squad leader. The company was out in a vineyard in foxholes, near Bebelheim, France. We had to stay in the foxholes all day, and at night we could get out. At night, Albert would stray out of the company area somewhere and goof off and get some liquor. He was drinking, and it was all I could do to contain him. The Germans would shoot screaming meemies artillery shells over and along with heavy 88 shelling. This had no effect on us, whatsoever. It didn't worry us one way or the other.

On December 23rd, the Germans had control of a bridge. It was to our right front, 3000 yards. Since I had been to rest camp, I was selected to go on a patrol. Our objective was to go find the enemy's strength on this bridge, because it was important to know this. I was made the first scout on the basis I was single. Dossi was second scout. We began our mission and Dossi said, "I can't make you be the first scout all the time, Craft. I'll go part of the time as first scout and you go part of the time." We had been told there was a river we could follow. We weren't on the banks, but stayed away from there to prevent silhouetting ourselves. We had on a white sheet that covered our helmets down to our boots. We got down to a wooded area and Dossi and I were alternating positions of scouts. I was going along, and all of a sudden, I had to go up an embankment. I didn't realize it was a road bed, because of the snow.

I climbed up to the top, and I heard Germans talking and almost stepped out on the road. I heard two Germans coming down the road. I stepped back quietly and quickly and melted down in the snow face down. I watched those Germans go by. I could have reached out and touched them as they passed by, but instead I slid down the bank and went back to talk to Sergeant Stern. We heard a machine gun click and a tank crank up and then a German ambulance came down the road and went off to the left into a little town.

When we heard that, we knew that they had it fortified due to the fact there was traffic and there were Germans. We heard the machine guns click when we made a noise. We also heard several tanks crank up warming their motors. We went back and reported to Battalion Headquarters that the bridge was heavily defended. Remember, this was on December 23, 1944.

On Christmas Eve, (the next night), Sergeant White said we had to go back down on a 12 man combat patrol and knock the bridge out. I didn't want to be a scout so I volunteered to be the grenadier. I had some grenadier attachments for my rifle and grenadier grenades. I also had some flares in the event we got into trouble. We were supposed to shoot red flares in that kind of situation. When the artillery saw the red flares, they would support us. We got down near the bridge, and the Germans were lying in wait for us. They opened up on us. We didn't want to engage with them due to our small number. Backing off and running up the field, I shot the red flares and fell down until they went out. Our artillery never came, and the Germans followed us back to our lines. We got through our lines safely, after a furious argument over our identity. The poor guys on those outposts really had a time chasing the Germans off. We reported this to Battalion Headquarters.

The Air Corps was called in on the bridge, and the next day about 300 bombers came over our foxholes and we could see bombs headed toward the bridge. They were also bombing other targets across the river. When the bombs exploded, we could feel the earth quivering, even though we were two miles away.

Lo and behold, the next night, Christmas night, they wanted three men from the 1st Platoon to go back to see if the Air Corps had really knocked it out. Albert, Silks and myself were called upon to go. The reason they wanted me to go was that they wanted someone that had been down there before and knew the way. I was complaining about three nights straight on patrol. It wasn't fair! We got almost down to the bridge. There was a ditch dug across a field we had encountered two times before. We had a conference and decided that one man should be left behind in the ditch to guard the rear, while the other two went to check the bridge. Silks and Albert decided it was better for me to stay in the ditch. Five or 10 minutes after they left me, I heard big guns shooting off in the rear, our 155's, and Silks and Albert were out there on the bridge, and the bridge was the 155's target. They were coming over me so low, I thought they were going to cut my head off. They gave it such a heavy shelling, I thought that they had gotten Silks and Albert, but I kept waiting for them. Finally, not knowing how much time had elapsed, they came. They said the shells had hit close by them, but they got in German foxholes and that is the only thing that saved them. We went back without any further incident, and as we were going into our lines, there was an outpost. The man on guard was drinking, and he hollered "Halt." Leading the way, I didn't hear, and he shot at me. That stopped me, and I really cussed him out. He told us to advance and be recognized. We did, and we really crawled all over him. I really told him off, because it was bad enough to be shot at by the Germans, and then have to face the fear of our own shells, too, and then to be challenged and shot at by our own man. We chewed him out for awhile. Then we went back and reported the bridge destroyed, and how we were shelled by our own artillery. We stayed in this vineyard a few more days. By that time, Albert was really getting drunk and unruly. He'd found more liquor to drink and had gone up to the CP and cursed them all out, including company commander, Lieutenant Sauer, and everyone in authority. He behaved terribly, and I considered Albert a friend. I did my best to calm him down, trying to talk him out of his mood. You couldn't reason with him, because he had reached the point where he couldn't take any more combat.

He was eliminated as squad leader, leaving us without one. I forgot to mention, that we did not get Christmas dinner, as folks in the States were told by the media. This was two holiday meals that we missed.

We were put on trucks and taken some distance. We were asked if any of us had any experience with animals. Farm boys! They wanted somebody to take burrows on the mountain, hauling concertina wire and supplies. I volunteered immediately, because I had experience with animals, but it never did materialize. The Ghoums kept the job.

We were going on a mountain and we went up on a hill to relieve the Algerian division, whom we called "Ghoums." The American soldiers looked terrible, but the Ghoums, because they are different from us, looked worse. On our way, marching to this hill 1415, we were going through very deep snow. It was very tiring, and it really tested our strength. We reached the point where we were going to turn up the mountain. A couple of Ghoums said to me, "You'll never make it. You're too soft." I ignored them, and we went up and exchanged positions with some of the other Ghoums. While there we were told there was a road we could go through with safety and a path from that road to our foxhole. If we got off this path, we would be blown to bits, because it was heavily mined.

I shared an outpost foxhole with a fellow named James Blattery from San Diego, California. It was a good foxhole. We both could lie down at one time, if we so desired. It had a good covering, with timber and dirt thrown on top of it. A deep snow had covered it. Some of the foxholes had hay in them to make it warmer. However, the hay was infested with fleas. It was real, real cold. Our whole company was so thinly spread out, although we were very much in demand, and had to defend 1,000 yards.

The foxhole closest to us had been manned by one man with a .50 caliber machine gun. I don't know how he managed that or what his tactics were. I know they fought in a very different fashion from us. The Ghoums are something between a black and white man. They had course black hair. They spoke French. Some could speak broken English, and they liked to be admired. Some GIs were talking to one, after we got on top of the hill. All of the Ghoums carried knives in a leather sheath attached to their cartridge belt. One GI asked a Ghoum to let him look at his knife. Apparently, this was a prized possession of this Ghoum. But after everyone admired it and handed it back to him, he took the knife and made a slit in his finger, took the blood and rubbed it over the blade, wiped it off with a handkerchief. When asked why he did this, he said, "We never draw our knife from the sheath, unless we use it and have spilled blood." He put the knife back in his sheath. That ended this event.

We were on this hill from December 30, 1944, until January 17, 1945. It was very distressing and bitter cold. The Germans were shelling us with their 88's. On the outpost where I was, they shelled it unmercifully. We dived down into the hole. As soon as it would let up, we'd jump out, poke our head out, look around to see if we could see the Germans coming, because we were fearing a counter-attack. The way our defensive positions were set up, we had a walking patrol that went down this trail every hour during the day and night, in spite of the fact that we had a telephone.

You can imagine every time the Germans would shell our position, 50 percent of the time, it would knock our telephone out. There were many, many experiences that we had during these 18 days, while we were up on the mountain. Blattery, who was my foxhole buddy, must have been five or six years older than me. He seemed to be a personable fellow. However, he seemed to have a desire to be promoted. Although younger than he, I had more guts than he did. One night, we had taken a severe shelling, and it quieted down. We heard some mines explode. I jumped up, got on the phone and was telling the CP about the mine exploding, so Blattery grabbed the phone out of my hand and began to try to explain in detail what was happening. I think he made a hit with the captain, because he seemed to be the logical one to go up as a squad leader. However, he never did make it. Anyway, that didn't bother me. I didn't want to be a squad leader or anything. I wanted to come home. Our feet were cold. From the time I left the rest camp, I hadn't changed socks. I had to come back from the rest camp a day or two before Christmas and now it was a week into January. My feet were cold, and we were getting a lot of frostbite. I thought sure I was going to come down with frozen feet, too. It was almost unbearable for us to live out in this snow, especially under the pressure of being shelled and pulling patrol duty. We were getting rations, which were cold. The only thing we got hot was instant, hot, black coffee. Instant coffee I detest to this day.

When we first moved up Hill 1415 the contact patrol consisted of two men, one of whom was a boy named Shelps from Virginia, and he spoke with a Virginia brogue. For the word "about," a—b—o—u—t, he pronounced it "a—b—o—o—t."

When they were coming down the trail, the Germans sent in a terrific barrage of 88s, and they were falling on the trail and all around our foxholes. I was leaning on my knees out in the foxhole with my head out. I had my gun positioned to shoot. I was peeping out of the foxhole. All of a sudden, while the shelling was still continuing, the figure of a man hurled through the darkness and I almost pulled the trigger. However, he was so fast, he dived in on top of both Blattery and I, and by that time, we knew it was a GI. It really, really frightened me, because I had almost killed him. I said, "Good God, Shelps, can't you do better than that? You know I almost killed you." He replied, "Aw, shut-up, Craft. I'm not worried about that damn little pea-shooter you have. I'm more concerned about those big ones, the 88's." I retorted, "Well, you'd be just as dead from this little M-1 bullet, as you would be from an 88. And if that ever occurs again, I'll pull the trigger next time." I really took him to task about it, but he didn't seem to mind. Really, old Shelps was yellow, and he was scared to death. If I had been in his position though, I don't know what I would have done. They got up and went on their way, contacting their regular schedule. We could hear our tanks moving around to different positions and this doggone tank got near our position or behind us. We couldn't see him, but could hear him, and we knew he was pretty well in line with us. Then he'd start shooting. No sooner than he'd shoot a few rounds, the Jerry artillery would answer him. A lot of those shots would fall short and hit around us. Blattery and I cursed those tanks unmercifully, but it didn't change the picture. They still continued to do it.

We had been there several days when the artillery had slackened. Things had kind of quieted down, and we'd been issued fur caps for our steel helmets — a cap that would come down over our ears. I pulled my helmet off, not realizing that this cap, while not the same color, was similar to the ones that the Germans wore. Usually when the Germans surrendered they didn't have their helmets on, only the cap. We were very familiar with their cap, and it was absent—mindedness, but as I was going down the trail with my rifle, I looked up and saw 10 or 15 GIs led by old Dossi. They were coming after me, yelling like Indians. I hollered at them, and they didn't hear me. I thought that they were going to shoot me. I dived into a ditch. They came up, had their guns pointed at me, saying, "Good God, it's you, Craft." I said, "Yeah, you silly sons-of-a-bitch, you Dossi, you of all people, come running at me with a damn gun."

He said, "Well, I thought you were a damn Kraut. You ought to have your helmet on, Craft." He and I exchanged a few words. Neither of us won. However, I felt kind of sheepish, for I understood their position. We got that patched up, and I went back and put my helmet on.

I went back along the trail, down to the command post to get some rations. It had gotten dark by this time and everything was very still. The Germans had a loudspeaker somewhere in the valley, or on the other mountain. I don't know where they were, but they had the volume turned up where we could hear it, and they were playing hillbilly songs on a record and saying on the loud speakers, "Yankee, go home. There's another man sleeping with your wife." Their purpose was to demoralize us. They attempted the same thing when propaganda leaflets were dropped and when they shot screaming meemies at us. It didn't have the effect on us that they thought it would. In fact, it made us angry. I picked up some mail and rations. Before I left the company command post, our artillery opened up and shut the Germans' music up.

Before we left this position, one night I was called on to go on another combat patrol. There were about 12 or 15 of us. We were supposed to go out and get a German prisoner. They had a platoon sergeant from the 3rd Platoon, who was a Yankee Dago. He was afraid of his own shadow. I was, too! I think everyone was, but I know as long as I was in authority over the other men, I never did display any yellowness or reluctance to carry out an order. One of the fellows with us was old Bagsdale from Texas. We got in a huddle and were told what was expected of us. We had to go through our lines down to another place through another platoon. We stopped there and talked with those boys to find out what the situation was in that particular sector. We headed down the mountain through the snow. We went a long way. I was a private first class with a little over two months combat experience. Nobody paid any attention to me. I didn't have any say on where we were going, how we were going to do it, or what. I had to go along and do my part.

This little sergeant got cold feet. After we had gone a good distance, he stopped us all. We got in a huddle and he said, "You know this is useless to be going on this patrol. Let's go back and tell them that we ran into the Germans and had a fire fight and couldn't do anything with it and had to retreat. We couldn't get a German prisoner." We'd been up there a long time. It was cold. We didn't feel like fighting, especially not on patrol. We all agreed and went back. Going back through the foxhole, we stopped to talk with the guys and this sergeant was telling what we had done. We hadn't actually gone on patrol. Old Bagsdale, unknowing to us, was in that foxhole and he listened to every word that the sergeant was telling those guys. They didn't say anything either. We counted our men and found that one was lost and it was Bagsdale. The sergeant was angry about Bagsdale and said he was going to report him. One day over the telephone, I heard old Bagsdale talking to somebody else. He was bragging that he really had the sergeant, if he reported him for not going on patrol. He would report what he overheard and would get the sergeant in trouble, too. I told Bagsdale he was a yellow son-of-a-bitch and if he reported it, he could figure on getting gut shot, because some of us were going to do it. Fortunately, the sergeant never did report him and I don't know what was quite right. I know the rest of us would have gone on patrol had the sergeant not taken his action, but this thing died down. It was useless and senseless to risk 13 men's lives on a deal like that. That is the only time that type of thing ever happened where I was involved, but it must have occurred many times.

I have never mentioned this fellow, Jones, from Florida. He came back to the outfit shortly before we crossed the Meurthe River. His complexion was yellow. He had yellow jaundice, which is a liver disease quite common with men having to live out in the manner in which we were forced to live. All of us guys had always talked of being wounded, where we would have it made and be shipped back to the States, and we could tell when we were kidding. It wasn't really an obsession with us, but it was with Jones. One afternoon, I heard one lone rifle shot. Everybody was interested, because it could have been an attack by the Heinies.

I got on the telephone to find out what it was and I was told that Jones had shot himself in the foot. I knew doggone well that it wasn't an accident. I knew he did that deliberately. The medics took him to an ambulance and we never saw Jones again.

Before we left these positions, Sergeant Grayson came up to check on the letter that he'd ask me to write to Wallace Clark. I explained to him that I had written the letter and when I got through we were told that we were moving out. I went down to the company command post to give it to him, but they had already packed up and gone. He said, "Yes, that's right; they had." He said, "Do you still have the letter?" I told him yes and pulled it out of my pocket. It was muddy and damp. Ink had faded a little on the envelope or water marks were on it. He took and sealed it and said he'd mail it and he understood the delay.

In the next day or two, we were told to bring our guns and all our belongings, which wasn't too much, and report back to the company area. We were told that we were going to leave these positions; someone else was going to relieve us. We were going on the other side of the mountain to defend it. It was the 254th Regiment from the 63rd Division, who was assigned to us. A day or two before, they had had their engineers up in our area hunting for mines. They were demining the place. The Ghoums had put them out, and they didn't know where they were. They had to find them by mine detector. I know one poor guy was following it and had the mine detector in his hand. The Germans had a plastic mine and it wouldn't detect, and the poor guy stepped on it. It was their shoe mine and it went off tearing his foot off. This was another terrible experience we had to witness. It was so close, less than five or six feet from the path to our foxhole.

When we were back in the company area, we were told that we were going on the other side of the mountain. Albert and I were foxhole buddies again. We were the farthest out, closest to the Germans, like we had been before. This time we got a real big foxhole with a good shelter on it, and we could move around. About 100 or 200 yards back to our rear was another foxhole with two more guys in it. We had a telephone and could talk to the platoon CP. We had a second lieutenant as a platoon leader, but I have forgotten his name. They changed so fast, it was difficult to keep up with them. They seemed able to go back to the hospital for small things — maybe he had bad breath or constipation. We seldom had a platoon leader with us in combat. It was always a sergeant and Albert was very jittery. Regimental Headquarters decided to send two companies out of the 3rd Battalion on a battle patrol and go down and make an experiment to see what the Germans had. They came out through our outpost, and we could hear the shooting. Boy, they really had a fight and lost a lot of men, killing some Germans and capturing some. From that moment, Albert began worrying. He said, "They are going to go down there and make those Krauts mad. They will follow them back to our lines." I said, "Aw, no, maybe not, Albert." "Yeah, they are." So he'd gotten me jittery, too. Albert said he wanted to go back to check with the other outpost behind us. I told him, "All right." He was gone for a long time.

He didn't come back and I went to find Albert. I said to him, "Albert, it's awful lonesome up there by myself."

He says, "I don't care. I'm not going back, Craft."

I said, "You've got to. I've got to have some help."

He replied, "No, those Germans are going to follow the combat patrol."

He wouldn't come back with me. I called Sergeant White and told him the set up. He said, "Well, Craft, stay by yourself." I did it, but it was rather lonesome there. I couldn't get any sleep, because I was afraid the Germans would slip up on me. We stayed there several days, and I began to hear a German artillery gun shooting. It would shoot, hitting over the hill towards my left. White and the lieutenant were across the valley from me and I got them on the phone and told them, "I can hear this gun when it shoots." They were shelling an outpost at another angle across the valley. These guys were reporting that they were being shelled, and I heard them talking to White. I identified myself and said, "I know where the shelling's coming from. It's down here to my right, and you wait until he shoots again." He was shooting, and then stopped for an interval, then he would shoot again. When he would shoot again, I said, "Now, here it comes."

Sure enough, the guys over there at the foxhole said, "Yes, that's the shell that just landed right here around us." That went on for some time. He shelled and I would tell them when it was being shot. They couldn't hear it, but I could. I must have been pretty close. The shell would drop around them. I don't know how long we stayed there, but we got orders to pack up and leave our foxholes and assemble back to our other area, where the platoon sergeant was.

It was night when we got over there, and we were told that we were being pulled off the mountain. I walked down the mountain, and along the side, over to where White and the platoon CP was and we went to the company area, and joined our company. We merged with the other platoons, and then went back over the mountain. Between our original positions on this, there was a German machine gun squad artillery had gotten, and all five of them were dead. You could see where the shells had hit. That was a terrible sight to see, but a sweet relief. We knew five more Germans and one machine gun would not shoot at us again. We got back to a warehouse, and like all warehouses, it wasn't heated, but it was better than being out in the cold. It provided shelter. We had found some metal containers and coal. We built a fire to keep warm. Each platoon had a coal fire in their platoon area. I don't know how we managed this, but that was exactly how we got heat. There didn't seem to have been too much smoke. As I told you, my friend Blattery, whom I pulled a few days with in the foxhole and this guy, Albert really disliked one another. Albert couldn't take combat any more, and was on the outs with me, but he still respected me. He had no respect for Blattery at all, because Blattery, as I intimated before, wanted to get some kind of promotion.

There was a group of us sitting by the fire one night, and Blattery was there, too. He would take Albert to task on any subject. It made Albert mad. He managed to get a hold of some wine or cognac, and Albert pulled out two M-1 .30 caliber cartridges and threw them into the blazing fire. Everybody ran for fear the shells would explode. Albert backed off a little, but I stayed near the fire, really not knowing what to do. I didn't want Albert to get in trouble. I don't know why I did this, other than maybe I wanted to keep Albert from getting reprimanded or court-martialed. I reached in with my hands real quick and grabbed the shells out one at a time, before they got hot and exploded. After I did, Blattery and the rest of the guys came back, and Albert said to Blattery, "Well, now, Blattery, you see who the brave one is now. And who's got the guts. It's Craft. You notice, he didn't duck. He reached over there and got the shells out." That seemed to have the desired effect on Blattery. He was quiet from then on.

We went out the next day. We were there two or three, maybe four days. We went on a march and practiced shooting with our rifles. We threw some grenades and then we shot our rifles. I was chosen to shoot a rifle grenade. The way this was done, you put a blank cartridge in your rifle chamber, and attached the grenade on the end of your rifle and shot at your target. You didn't aim like you did when you ordinarily were shooting with bullets. You estimated the distance and tilted your rifle towards the target. You'd call this the "Kentucky Windage." I shot the target three times and got a bull's eye. I was told to fire two or three more, which I did, and each time I hit the target. I just seemed to have a knack for that type of thing. I was the grenadier, for a while, for my squad.

One day, we marched out into a large field, outside of a town named Hacimette. This is where they held war medal ceremonies, and General O'Mike Daniel came to conduct this award and gave us a pep talk. The field was covered with snow. We either rode over by truck or we walked, but we thought it was kind of silly to be getting out in that kind of weather for this type of thing. He began to tell us what a glorious job we had done, and the 3rd Division was known for its reputation of never having been in defensive positions, and that we were anxious to get out and kill some more Bosch. He knew everybody felt the same way. Well, that was contrary to our thinking. We were simply tired of the whole situation, and we wanted to go home. This type of thing didn't hit off too well. The whole regiment, when he started that kind of talk, simply booed him, and if you can, imagine a regiment of soldiers booing their commanding general. Order was eventually established. He made his speech short, and then he left. We went on back to the warehouse and stayed there another night. When we started moving up to our jump off place at Bebelheim, France, we were going to take Ostheim, France. It was under cover of darkness, and at 2100 (about 9:00 p.m. that night) on January

22, 1945, the 1st and 3rd Battalions crossed the LaFecht River on a bridge and the 1st Battalion's mission was to capture Ostheim, France.

If I may back up a little — before we crossed this river, a few days prior, Lieutenant Mahaffey, who had us in basic training in Fort McLelland, had joined our outfit and was the platoon leader of the 2nd Platoon of Charlie Company, whom Johnny Clayton was with. Johnny was chosen to go on patrol to swim the LaFecht River. It was Mahaffey with three or four other men. Snow was on the ground and the temperature was freezing. They swam the river and Mahaffey stayed near the river bank, where he could get back across and escape easily, should the enemy attack. He had Johnny Clayton walk on a dike across the field to draw fire from the Germans.

Mahaffey says, "There's no Germans here," and Johnny told him, "Yes, there is. I can smell them." Mahaffey scoffed at that, and had Johnny walk across the field again on the dam. Johnny was silhouetted, and a perfect target for the Germans. Had the Krauts wanted to, they could have shot Johnny down, but they chose not to.

Johnny walked up across it several times and told him, "Lieutenant, there's Krauts here. I can smell them."

The lieutenant said, "Aw, there's not a German within miles." They swam back across the river and put some fresh clothes on. They had all been promised a fifth of American whiskey when they got back to warm them up.

Lieutenant Mahaffey went to the company CP and reported no Germans in the vicinity and obtained five fifths of American whiskey. The enlisted men, after changing their clothes, met at Lieutenant Mahaffey's tent to get their whiskey. He had opened a bottle and had taken several drinks and attempted to pass it around to each of the fellows for a drink. He began with Clayton, and Johnny said to him, "Lieutenant, I don't want your whiskey. I came for my bottle." The lieutenant insisted, and Clayton said, "Lieutenant, we were promised a fifth of American whiskey. We earned it! I don't want yours, just mine, and if I don't get it, I'll gut shoot you." Realizing that Clayton would shoot, he pretended that he just wanted to drink and share, but Clayton wouldn't fall for this, and each member of the patrol went back to his tent, with a fifth of whiskey.

Back to January 22, 1945, at 9:00 PM: I no longer served as a scout. Snow was knee deep, since it had been snowing since November 10th or 11th continously and this was late January. We never saw any pretty or warm days. (It kept on snowing on top of snow). There were high drifts hip deep. It is hard to identify ditches or things of that nature, unless it was a huge ditch. We reached the point where we made contact with the enemy, who opened up on us with machine gun fire. We took the nearest cover. There was a depression in the ground; you could tell, in spite of the snow. It was a ditch. Everybody headed for its cover. The Germans used good judgment in this respect. They knew it was the first place that we'd head for, and they had mined the ditch. Several people jumped in, and got blown up. There were people that sat down on mines, blowing them up. It was chaos! Colonel Collen was there with us. He encouraged us to go on. We jumped out of the ditch and headed for the machine gun. Somehow, we managed to knock it out. That wasn't primarily my company's objective. However, several machine guns were silenced. We got into a wooded area, traveled for a short distance and found a trail. No sooner than we did, contact was made with the Germans again.

There was a German pillbox in the middle of the woods, near the trail. We threw in a barrage of rifle fire and asked them to come out. They wouldn't surrender. We had them so unnerved. We were shooting bazookas, throwing grenades, and finally one German came out crying. He had his hands up. He'd come a little way and then go back. We could hear another German talking to him. Apparently, it was an officer making him come back. This Kraut soldier wanted to surrender. I hollered for the German captain to surrender, who replied, "Yank, come and get me." I answered, "I'm not a damn Yankee, I'm a Rebel. Come on out with your hands up." Again, this soldier got out of the pillbox and was trying to surrender. I was standing directly across the trail from him. I thought he was surrendering, but he pulled out a pistol and shot at me point blank. He wasn't far from me, just across the trail, maybe 10 to 12 feet. He shot and missed. Then he ran back into the pillbox. When he did that, he made everybody fighting mad. I'm telling you, we cut down on them with everything we had.

CHAPTER 14
ON THE BATTLEFIELD

While this was going on, Officer Collen came up and said, "Let B Company handle this." He wanted A and C Companies to go into Ostheim. We proceeded on toward Ostheim.

We were hitting fragments of resistance and got to the edge of town. There was a German tank, which began shooting at us. We drew some machine gun fire, too. We came to a wall and found a lost American soldier. He came up to us and wanted to know if we were B Company. Some of us were trying to tell him where it was. We had just left them, but he was welcometostaywithus.OfficerCollensaid,"Youyellow son-of-a-bitch, you didn't have any business getting lost. I've a good mind to shoot you." If Collen had done that, he would have never lived to tell the story. I'm sure, myself, and I know Sergeant White, my good friend from Elizabethton, along with many others, would have shot Collen down, but old Collen bemeaned the guy and abused him verbally. The poor fellow left crying. He was in a terrible position. He should have been allowed to stay with us. The very fact that he got lost from his company, with as much confusion as there was, didn't require that kind of treatment. The man left, and we never knew what happened to him. That was the first time I wanted to shoot Collen. There were a couple of other times that I felt like it. Many others felt the same way, too.

This tank kept maneuvering and finally, we got a bazooka team out and started shooting at the tank. We were going to close in on him, because we didn't have any tanks with us at that time. The German tank kept backing off, and finally it fled. Then we proceeded to clear the town. We worked all night clearing Ostheim. The next morning, we found a cellar where we could stay. Every time we'd try to get out of the cellar and on to the street, there was a sniper shooting. He was shooting with a burp gun. All of us thought he was shooting from the church steeple, which is pictured in the 7th Infantry's history book. The reason we couldn't knock that particular steeple down is because we didn't have any tanks. Our tanks couldn't cross. They tried to, but the bridge collapsed underneath the lead tank. They ran out of material to build bridges. How they even built a bridge in that kind of weather, I don't know. It rocked on until 5:00 PM in the evening. The sniper finally quit.

We got orders to pull out. We didn't know where we were going. We were told that the 2nd Battalion had run into some heavy resistance, and they had been severely crippled and we had to go to their rescue. We walked, walked and walked. Before we left, we didn't have a BAR man (Browning

Automatic Rifle). I told Sergeant White, I'd take it. I didn't really know what I was getting into, because the ammunition you had to carry with the rifle was prohibitive for a man my size. It was really a burden, carrying that load bogging through the snow. I managed to keep up with the platoon. We went through the woods until we got to a clearing. It was a field. As we were looking out of the woods, we could see a huge fire burning. They apparently had three haystacks and were shooting phosphorous shells into them, igniting the hay. The flame was going 20 to 50 feet in the air. The circumference of the bonfire was probably 15 feet and the whole open area was well lit. They repeatedly shot phosphorous shells into the hay to give them light. We pulled up at the edge of the woods. We had a conference and started across the field. I don't remember how we lined up, only that C Company went across, the 1st and 2nd Platoons went together, with the 3rd Platoon in reserve behind us, along with the weapons platoon, which consisted of the mortars. Our machine gunners were with us. We started across the field and noticed the machine guns were shooting slowly, because we could see the tracers. They had a criss-cross fire, and we had to go across it. The field was approximately 500 yards wide. When we got more than half way, or nearly across, the interlacing machine gun fire was being fired at pretty long distances, but the firing intensified, and we got the machine gun fire from directly in front of us, but we plunged on, with men being hit. We came to a small incline. I didn't recognize the road at the time, but it was a highway bed. We climbed up, got on top, ran across the road and down another incline with a ditch, then a wooded area. There was a barb wire fence. We climbed through the barb wire fence, and got over and were getting ready to take off. Nebeney was a scout. He was an older man and a tough old bird. He went on out in front of us. I looked to my right and I saw a group — it looked like the Germans lined up. They opened up with their burp guns. All of them had burp guns. There must have been 15 or 20 of them. They were liquored up, on dope, and as they started opening up, I threw my BAR up to my shoulder and shot down the line. I'm not sure how many of them I hit, but it didn't stop them. No sooner than I fired a clip at them, a rifle grenade hit near me. A fragment of it got Tanner, a guy from New York City, in the eye. He became very indignant. I know it did hurt him; it was just a flesh wound, though, it could have put his eye out. He says, "Cut out firing that BAR." I don't know what he wanted us to do, because that was the only thing we could do. Sergeant White was in charge of the platoon. I think the sergeant was back in the ditch. Those Germans kept on coming, spouting those burp guns and murdering those poor guys. We were shooting back and forth and one German, who had to be liquored up, ran up and grabbed one of our machine guns out of a dead man's hand and put it on his shoulder.

We were really in a bad way. We were disorganized, we didn't know where we were, and Colen had been hit and was lying down across the calves of my legs. I was lying on the ground. This German turned around and filled Colen full of bullets. Not a one struck me. There were men crying. There was a boy from Florida, Colen's buddy, Leon. He was crying and carrying on. "Oh, Lord, we are going to be killed," and I dressed him down. I told him we had to fight and for him to quit being a baby. We could not take that attitude. It quieted him down, and those of us who could, moved into the ditch. There wasn't many of us left. My BAR would not fire anymore. I had two hand grenades left, and I had one with the pin out of it, and I had thrown the pin away, and I was holding this grenade.

There was a private, who was an aide to an artillery observer with us. He didn't know what to do. I said, "Soldier, I can't shoot with this grenade in my hand. I can't find the pin. Do you want to hold it?" The guy agreed to. I went over to the ditch and found Captain Maize and Sergeant White and got down in between them. I tried to talk to Captain Maize, and I couldn't get any response, just a grunt. So I talked to White, who had been hit, too. I asked him, "What's wrong with Captain Maize? I believe he's dead — dying," and he said, "He's been hit bad, Craft."

I said, "What are we going to do?"

He said, "I don't know."

I replied, "Well, they got us."

He said, "Yes, that's right; looks like they've got us."

No sooner had we talked, then the Germans set up a machine gun to fire down the ditch. In order to keep from being hit (I don't know why I thought of this), I lay flat in that ditch on my back with my legs up one bank and my head up the other bank. Those bullets went over me, but it got a lot more of those guys. Well, the firing ceased. The Krauts started coming up, close to where we were and throwing hand grenades on us. They would come back and say, "Come, surrender." There was one GI, who jumped up to surrender, with his hands up, and they shot him down.

I vowed then, that I wouldn't surrender. They kept on coming up throwing grenades in, and they threw one that exploded on my helmet. A fragment of it must have hit Troy White, because I heard him yelp. But my ears were ringing. I couldn't hear anything. The concussion shook me up. I don't suppose it really did me any harm, it certainly didn't do me any good, but I was in so much better shape than the rest of the people. I didn't have a gun that would shoot.

By that time, they were getting a little cautious and they'd come up — "Comrade, comin' a here, mit hands aho" and nobody would surrender. There were only six of us left. They tried these tactics for a while, kept throwing their grenades, and I said to White, "They've got us. We need to make a run for it, or somebody needs to make a run and try to get some help."

And he said, "That sounds like a good idea to me."

I said, "I've got one grenade here. When they come back and ask us to surrender, why don't I throw that grenade, and at that time, make a run for it?"

White replied, "That sounds like a good idea."

The Germans came again, about 15 feet from us and they tried to get us to surrender. I pulled the grenade out, pulled the pin and peeked out over the top of the bank, and I saw three Krauts standing together in a close circle and threw the grenade, and it landed in the middle of them. I know it was bound to have killed them. That grenade exploded like a cannon, and all I could see in a radius of about 15 feet around it was a ball of fire. White jumped up to the ditch bank with his rifle and he yelled, "Take off, Craft." I jumped up and ran to this wire fence. I climbed through it, crossed and examined the road. I saw about eight or 10 German tanks, but that didn't deter me. I kept running, and got out into the field; the machine guns opened up on me.

As soon as the firing began, I fell like I was dead. I lay there for a few minutes. All the ammunition and equipment I had on was weighing me down. I began to wiggle out of it. I had, at first, thrown my BAR down, and then got rid of the equipment. Jumping up, I really began to run. They opened up on me with everything they had — machine guns — enemy tanks were shooting at me point blank. I could feel the bullets whizzing by me. I had only one weapon with me that night, the Lord. He was with me many times before, I am sure, but especially this night in particular. Aware of the fact that I was being shot at by numerous machine guns and tanks, I called out to the Lord to help me. I ran again. They opened up fire again. I fell down like I was hit again. They stopped shooting. I jumped up, did this type of faking, until I was better than half way across the field. The German tanks started shooting at me, point blank. A shell went by me, that was like a ball of fire. It missed me. I was thinking that they were bound to get me the next time. Looking out ahead, I saw a bomb crater. Apparently, the Air Corps had been bombing this place. I jumped in it and stayed there for a little while, and things quieted down. I jumped up and began running. The shooting at me had ceased.

After running 500 yards, which is pretty taxing on anyone, especially in snow, I came close to the wooded area we had left when we jumped off. I was challenged by a GI, who wanted to know the password. We had not been given the password, or else I had so much happen to me that I couldn't remember it. The guy sounded pretty anxious, had his gun on me, and I said, "Say, fellow, I'm an American. Don't shoot me."

He replied, "What's the password?" I said, "I don't know the damn password." "I'll tell you what, Buddy. I'm from the State of Mississippi and

Mount Olive is my hometown. I've run out of a trap over there and my whole outfit has been wiped out. Put your rifle down and let me come on in and I'll explain to you."

He said, "Well, you can come in, but you'd better have your hands up and you better come slow, and don't make a quick move. If you do, I'm going to shoot you."

I proceeded cautiously, got up there and convinced him that I was a GI, and I think it was a damn sorry second lieutenant, who was a tank commander. I was telling him that I saw eight or 10 tanks that were at the edge of the woods, and that they knew the situation that we were in over there. They knew those German tanks were over there. I'm sure they did. I proceeded to tell them that the company commander had been killed and our whole company had practically been wiped out. Would they please go with me over there to get them — what was left?

He said, "No." They couldn't do that. They had to stay there.

We kept on talking and I said, "Well, look, you have all those tanks here, and you let us die over there. It's a sad state of affairs. If you want something to shoot at, there's about eight or 10 tanks across this field on the road, down there at the edge of the woods; all you've got to do is just shoot directly where I am pointing. Why don't you do that? You can knock them out." They couldn't do that. They had orders to stay right where they were and not shoot.

A few minutes later, the Krauts started laying artillery barrages on us. This lieutenant jumped up and went down into the tank and closed the hatch. I stood it long enough, then I jumped on the tank, and I beat on the hatch. He opened it up, raising it a little.

I said, "Lieutenant, please let me come in there with you. I don't have any protection."

He said, "No, you can't do it. It violates the rules."

I called him a lousy son-of-a-bitch, and saw that I didn't have a choice. Not having a gun or anything, I climbed down off the tank and got in between the treads for protection from the artillery. We stayed that way for a while. They kept shelling us pretty good. I heard a noise. I turned around and saw a column of men, I asked them who they were. They replied that they were C Company. I said, "C Company? C Company has been wiped out. Captain Maize has been killed. You can't be C Company."

"Oh, we're just the mortars."

I asked, "Who are you?"

And he said, "I'm Lieutenant Finch."

I replied, "Oh, lieutenant, I'm Craft with the 1st Platoon. I came back to get help."

He said, "Well, just fall in line at the end of the line."

I said, "I don't have a gun."

He said, "You can help one of the mortar men carry ammunition."

I went back to the end of the line and asked the young man if he wanted help carrying the ammunition. He had two sacks, one on each side. He gave me one of them. We went down to the edge of the woods a long way, crossed over the field, and tried to slip up on the Germans. They had their rear guarded and opened up on us with their machine guns. We tried to advance, but we couldn't. Finally, we decided to retreat and go back across the field. By then, it was beginning to get daylight. I walked up to Lieutenant Finch and asked, "Finch, where can I get a rifle?" By that time, we had come in contact with fragments of the 3rd Platoon. They hadn't crossed the field on the original assault.

He said, "They are a rifle platoon. Go and dig in with one of their men."

I replied, "I don't have a rifle."

He said, "That's all right." He called a sergeant, saying, "Buddy, put this man with one of yours." The sergeant did, and I started digging in with this guy. We had one shovel between us. We began digging a hole and we'd gotten it dug about six inches deep, maybe six feet long, and about a couple of feet wide, when the Germans sent in a big artillery blast. They knew exactly where we were, under the trees in the forest.

The shelling was so severe that everybody took cover. An 88 shell hit the tree above us. This guy that was digging at that time fell in on the bottom and I fell on top of him. I didn't have much protection; my body was protecting him. All of a sudden, I felt a hard lick in the right side of my back and a burning sensation with a lot of pain. There was a fragment of that shell, about 12 inches long, two inches wide and one half inch thick, that hit me. If it hadn't been almost spent, I wouldn't be here telling my story today. It went through all my clothes, made a big bruise and a small cut, and it bled a little. It hurt, burned from the hard lick and I felt as if someone had hit me with a sledge hammer. It frightened not only me, but everybody around me. They said, "Good God, fellow."

They started calling for the medics. I said, "Oh, please don't call the medics. I'm not hurt that bad."

"Yes, you are." There were so many wounded, they couldn't get a medic to me.

One guy said, "There's an aid station right behind here. Let me help you back there." And I did. We saw a long tent. It seemed to be about 100 feet long and it had row after row of wounded soldiers in it. I looked down and saw Sergeant White. He was in shock. He was pale and gray in the face and unconscious. I was trying to get White's attention to find out how badly he was hurt. A medic came up and told a bunch of us guys standing there, "If you've been wounded and you're still mobile, and you can make it, go over this little hill. There's a jeep down there waiting that will take you into the regular aid station." I told him I could go, and two or three other guys went with me. We got on that jeep, and the driver took off.

Before I got to the jeep, I saw my good friend, Johnny Clayton, with his rifle slung over his shoulder. He was going to join our company. He saw me and said, "My gosh, Craft. What happened to you?"

I told him, "Johnny, I got hit. Our whole company is practically wiped out."

He came over and looked at me and said, "Gosh, you look terrible. Are you hurting? Can I do anything for you?"

I replied, "No, Johnny. I'm supposed to get on this jeep, and go back to the aid station."

He said, "Well, Craft, old buddy, I got lost from the company last night, but I'll tell you what, when I get back up there I'm going to get a few Krauts for treating you this way," to which I said, "Okay, Johnny. Get them, buddy; take care of yourself."

He said, "Craft, you take care of yourself, too." Then I got on the jeep. The driver spun the motor to life and rushed us to the aid station.

I must admit, I wasn't a good spectacle to look at. Everybody thought from the looks of my clothes, which they did have a little blood on them, that I was hurting badly. I got in the aid station, which was in a warm house. The doctor had me pull my coat and my shirt off, and let my underwear down. He looked at my back, not touching me, but quickly applied a bandage and said, "Soldier, your wound is not all that bad. I can tell by looking at you, that what you need is a long rest, but I can't give it to you. They are just too short of men up there. I'm going to have to send you back to the front."

I replied, "Well, Doc, that's all right. I'll go back, but I don't have a gun. I don't have any ammunition."

He said, "There is plenty of it around this aid station. Pick one up, and get some ammunition, wherever you can find it."

I said, "Okay."

Nothing was said about rations. By that time, I realized how hungry I was. My back was beginning to stiffen up on me. This was back in the town of Ostheim, we had captured two nights previously. I suddenly remembered — I couldn't find any rations. I thought, I bet you there are some rations down at the place where we jumped off from. I went back down there and did find some. I walked in and saw about six or eight guys. Most of them were from my platoon. There was Woodgate, Bagsdale, Albert, Blue and Shelps. They began to ask me about the company. I said, "Well, there ain't no more Charlie Company. Sergeant White was hit bad and Captain Maize was killed; they wiped us out. As far as I know, I am the only one that got out of the 1st and 2nd Platoon, except Sergeant White. I saw him at the aid station." My back was turned to them. I was sitting down on a can or a box.

They had a fire going and they asked, "You want something to eat?"

I replied, "Heck yeah, I do."

They asked me, "What do you want?"

I said, "I want one of the K ration breakfasts."

Albert fixed me some breakfast. I lay down to sleep and used my helmet or something for a pillow. As I drifted off into a deep sleep, they noticed the blood and my torn clothing. They pushed, and continued to push, but I didn't wake up. They thought I was dying! They couldn't see how badly I was hurt.

They were shaking me, calling, "Craft, Craft, Craft, wake up." They were really concerned about me. I woke up and shook my head, because from all that exposure and the dreadful experience I had, I passed out. I don't know how long they let me sleep. After I finally recovered a little, they wanted to know, that if I was hurt — just how badly was I hurt?

I said, "I'm not hurt bad. I've been to the aid station and the doctor saw me, and said I had to go back."

They wanted me to tell them again who was left, and I told them I didn't think anybody was left. Everybody was killed. I told them what the doctor at the aid station said. I said, "Incidentally, what are you yellow bastards doing back here? You deliberately took off, didn't you? You know if you had been up there, this might not have happened. I'm going back and every last one of you is going with me. Get your stuff together, we're going now."

They kind of looked sheepish and dropped their heads and started getting their equipment. I led the way. As we were going back toward the aid station, the regimental sergeant major came out. I asked him, "Can you tell me which way to get to the Charlie Company, 1st Battalion?"

He said, "You go up that road, and it will take you to where they are. You'll be able to find them." He looked at me, saw how bad I looked, and observed my clothes, seeing the blood and torn garments. He said, "Soldier, you don't mean to tell me you're going back up there, do you?"

I said, "Yes, I'm going."

He asked, "What happened to you?" And I told him. He said if that had happened to him, he wouldn't go back up there. They couldn't drive him. He wouldn't blame me, if I didn't go back. He told me not to go. I said, "Well, they need us up there. I appreciate your concern, but I've got to go. I've got to get these men up there." He said, "Well, more power to you. I admire a fellow like you, but I still wouldn't go, if I were you."

I thanked him again, and I said, "Come on, boys."

We started down the road, toward an intersection. I was leading, and I saw an empty jeep coming. I flagged it and asked him, "Say, fellow, do you know where Charlie Company is?"

He said, "Yeah, I know where they are supposed to be. I can get you pretty close." I got up in the front seat. Another guy followed me. The rest of them got on the jeep and hung on where they could find room. He began driving. And did he drive! Remember, there was snow on the ground, and he was driving fast. He took us into the Chateau D. Schoppenwilhr, that horrible place, where the Germans had fought so bitterly and practically wiped us out. We arrived there, got some coffee, asked the guy in charge how we could get to C Company. He said, "Well, C Company, you can't get to right now. But you fellows wait around here and when it gets night, I'll send somebody up to show you the way."

I don't know what time it was, only that it was getting pretty close to night. The Chateau D. Schoppenwilhr was a fancy castle. The Germans didn't want to give it up. We began to talk to the GIs there, and heard a few smattering details of what had happened there and whiled away the time. About dark, we started out to find Charlie Company. We found them in an old railroad station with a long open dock. I got out and reported in, and the 1st Platoon was in this building. There weren't many! Silks was there and also a lieutenant with a gold tooth and dark skin, a Hispanic.

The set up was that they had a pill box in front of the building we were in. As soon as I got up there, they put me on guard. I think I had to pull about four to six hours by myself. This pill box was in front of us. They had closed off one side. We had heavy machine guns, light machine guns, and we were looking for the Germans to come across the field from all directions. We were told that we had to guard this pill box. On the right side, if anybody came and went out of it, it was all right not to shoot. But if we saw any activity, whatsoever, on the left side, we were to shoot without question, because it would definitely be the Germans.

This lieutenant came out to check on me, to see whether I was pulling guard or not. We began talking and, thinking that I was a rookie, he related to me what had happened the night before. "You know, those Germans were crazy. They were drunk and doped up." I already knew the story, because I was in it, but he continued, "Just before daylight, there was some soldier that threw a grenade and that was the most perfect throw I have ever seen."

I replied, "Lieutenant, I'm that soldier." I don't think he believed me. It really didn't make any difference."

He repeated, "That was the most perfect throw. It landed right in among those three Germans."

That gave me a lot of satisfaction, because I had thought to myself that it was a perfect throw. I didn't try to convince the lieutenant anymore. I think he became embarrassed and left. Do you know he went back in the pill box where it was warm? He went in the right side, where we weren't shooting. Then all of a sudden my duty was to look out that way and look to our right flank. Quite suddenly, the heavy machine guns opened up, and when the shooting died down, I saw a flash of light. They apparently pulled this old bird in. They called for the medics to come and get him from the Chateau. I don't know how far the Chateau was. I'll never forget that name as long as I live, because of the horrible experiences I had. The medics came, and it was a while before they could get the stretcher bearers to get him.

But do you know who it was? It was this same lieutenant. His name was Gragg. What he had done, he'd gone into this warm CP and got nosy, and pushed that door, he wasn't supposed to open, and stepped outside. That heavy machine gunner let him have it. I understand he died later. There were some Germans who tried to get into the pill box. We were shooting at them and they ran back. One Kraut got pretty close, then chickened out and ran. I don't know whether he got away. I think we hit him.

Sometime during that night they pulled us back. We trudged down across this field as a group, and organized as well as could be. We went back to this Chateau, and I ran into Johnny Clayton. I ran into somebody else first. They were telling me in the 2nd Platoon: "That Johnny Clayton is a fantastic shot." It seems that they went across the field to take the Chateau and knocked out the enemy tanks. Collen had wandered off across the field somewhere and found an empty pill box, set up a CP, and the Germans had surrounded him. He was calling for artillery. He'd gotten on that radio and was literally crying, "They've got me surrounded. Get those men on the tanks to come down here and get me." And so that's what got the tanks moving. As Johnny related to me, they got on the tanks and waded out towards those other German tanks and machine guns, and it was this depot along with the Chateau, that the battalion captured. They got up there and our tanks were shooting them. They were trying to use bazookas against us, and old Johnny shot several of them.

A fanatical bunch of Germans got out, and rather than surrender, they were trying to escape. Old Johnny threw his M-1 up (I saw the bodies, and was told by people, other than Johnny) and picked them off like pigeons! I had some other fellows tell me. Johnny didn't admit it himself.

He just said, "Craft, I got even for you," the next time I saw him.

"I know you did, you rascal." So as we were pulling back towards the Chateau, they were really firing at those Germans. We passed the 4.2 mortars. Those things would burst your eardrums, almost when they shot. I don't know how the guys stood it.

Not only were they shooting 4.2's, they were shooting the 81 mortars, and the 105th Artillery guys were shooting. You could hardly hear yourself talk, or you could hardly think, but they apparently did a swell job in their shelling of the Germans. My hat was always off to the artillery people. I admired them very much, because they made a few mistakes, and I was a recipient of their mistakes. I'm sure for a fact the work that they did killed a lot of Germans.

CHAPTER 15
CROSSING THE CANAL DE COLMAR AND THE BIG FIGHT FOR THE JEWISH CEMETERY

We didn't stay long at Chateau De Schoppenwilhr. We were pulled back into a wooded area outside of Ostheim. Our officers made available the housing and pill boxes for themselves, so they could keep warm. All enlisted men had to dig foxholes in the woods. For covering over the foxholes, we got tree limbs; that was the shelter we had. There was an evergreen tree and it provided some shelter.

The next day, I got a letter from my sister, Irene, and she started off the letter, "Well, I hope you're still at the rest camp and enjoying it." That kind of annoyed me, because I had seen so much death and had been hit myself, and was just worn out. Sometime during the day, I scratched her a letter and told her that I had enjoyed the rest camp for three days, but this wasn't a rest camp over here. We had been fighting! We stayed there for a couple of days. They had pulled us back, to use us to cross another canal. It was the Canal de Colmar.

The only thing we carried in our packs was one or two blankets and we were told that we were going to cross this canal in boats. Regimental Headquarters thought it would be best if we turned in our packs and we'd get them back later on. I don't recall ever getting those packs back. We rested and were briefed a couple of days, there in the woods, then we were loaded into trucks and taken a distance. I don't know how far or in which direction. Then we were put out behind the lines, walking on up to the boats that were provided by the engineers. We'd been told that every sixth man had to carry the boats, probably a mile, and that's why they didn't want us to carry our packs. The canal was out in the open and we had to carry the boats from a place of concealment. We jumped off at 2100 and picked up our boat, put it in the canal, got in it, and paddled across and got out safely. We experienced a little resistance, but B Company was on our left, and was dispatched to get it. Charlie Company and Able Company proceeded on into Bischwihr. We met some opposition and ran over them. Finally, we had this town cleared about 3:00 a.m. in the morning. We found us a house, and our platoon had an area to hold.

By this time, I was a squad leader, and we'd gotten some new replacements in. I had one young fellow in my squad, who was my first scout. He took a liking to me, and I to him. He was so sincere and honest, I wish I could remember his name. He'd do anything in the world I'd ask him to do. I, likewise, would him, because we immediately trusted each other. I went out in the yard from our platoon CP. Being short of men, we had to post them by themselves to guard our area. As in a lot of cases, there were walls around the houses. The Krauts were shelling us furiously with the 88's.

While I was out there with this young man, shells began falling close to us. Two duds hit nearby and we were standing side by side. Another shell hit 15 feet from us, wounding both of us. My wound was not serious, as it was only a nick in the right calf of my leg, but the shell fragment was hot. This young man standing beside me was seriously injured in the leg. He thought I was, too. I called out for the medics and he told them to take care of me, as I was hit, too. I told the medic, that my wound was not serious. It was only a nick, but to take care of the young man. They put him on a stretcher, badly wounded, but he would not consent to being taken back to the aid station unless I went. The medics said it was not far away, and to pacify him, I accompanied them to the aid station.

When we arrived, they began their examination of him, but he insisted that I be treated first. Rather than antagonize him, they looked at my leg, treated it and put a bandage on it. This satisfied him and he allowed them to check his wound. He had a serious leg wound and had to be sent to the hospital. After treating his wound, they gave him a shot of morphine and he went to sleep. I really felt touched by this young man's confidence and loyalty. However, I was needed back on the lines and I left. One good thing came out of this. When the war was over, and the point system was established, this wound allowed me five points, because it was recorded in the medical records of the 3rd Battalion Aid Station.

We stayed there that night and until noon the next day. There was a wooded area that the reports indicated a lot of Germans were using to counter-attack. They shelled it heavily and had called upon the 1st Battalion to go to this wooded area. Bear in mind, we didn't have packs; ours had been turned in. We were going out in this forest without a blanket or a shovel to dig a hole. We walked into the snow covered forest and found the French troops there. We pulled up into the edge of the woods, overlooking the German positions. Those Frenchmen were coming up to assist us with their armour. They drove up with their headlights on, making loud noises, yelling to one another, blowing whistles, lighting cigarettes and some even had bonfires going, which was strictly against the rules, as far as we were concerned. We wouldn't light a cigarette unless it was well camouflaged, where the light couldn't be detected by the Germans.

We moved ourselves out into a defense position. It was bitter cold, and we didn't have a shovel or blanket. We couldn't dig in. The only thing we could do was use our hands and get limbs from some of the trees. We scooped the snow back and three of us would lie down together, close to one another as we could, and we'd alternate being the middle guy all during the night, so each of us could get our share of the warmth. We stayed there a day or two. We could see those Germans across the huge field down to our right, and we could see them moving materials, but we weren't there to fight, but to prevent them from using this to counter-attack.

We did do a little sniping at them. They knew we were up there and started shooting artillery. I remember one shell came in like a ball of fire and it bounced off a tree. It was like that shell that shot at me, when I was running out of the trap back at the Chateau. This shell hit a tree, bounced off, exploding and wounded a man from the 2nd Platoon. I didn't know who had been hit, but the medics came quickly. Then I went over to find out who was hit, and was told that it was Johnny Clayton. The Platoon Sergeant Loskey showed me the direction to the ambulance and I ran to catch up, but when I got there, the ambulance was gone. Now I was alone without a real close friend to fight the remainder of the war with. Johnny was the last one who started out with me, and I felt terrible.

The 75th Division came up and relieved us, and I was really amused. They had a second lieutenant in charge of the platoon that relieved us, who was fresh from the States, and wasn't battle wise. This second John, probably a 90 day wonder, didn't approve of our positions. He let it be known, our defense was not the way he would handle it, and was setting his defense better. I could care less how he handled it. I knew how we had to handle things, because we were handicapped. We didn't have shovels; we didn't have blankets. He and his men did, and they had been in a warm place. They were clean shaven and didn't look like they were hungry. I ignored this second lieutenant, and we pulled back to go back on the attack.

On or about February 1, we'd been marching along the road and were going to cross a canal. We got near it, and the Germans started letting us have it with artillery, mortars and machine gun fire. We had tanks with us. For tanks to be with us there had to be an anticipated heavy enemy resistance. I was following this tank through the woods with some other men and there were people on each side of us. When the artillery shells started to explode, the tank driver started backing up. There was a young man who was so tired he couldn't function properly, and he didn't get out of the way of the tank and it backed over him. I never will forget the death scream he gave as he was crushed beneath the tank. It was nerve racking to know that a life had been taken so needlessly by one of our own.

We retreated back to a road, then went to our right, up the canal, and crossed the bridge. We stayed for a few hours, and it was about daybreak. I know this was the same objective as before, where we got knocked back and couldn't cross. They told us that there was a Jewish cemetery at the end of this long field to our left. Our 3rd Battalion was having a hard time up at Biesheim, and from all indications they certainly must have. The Germans had a lot of tanks, infantry, artillery, anti-tank guns, and they were prepared to fight for it. When those poor guys with the 3rd Battalion got there the Krauts really let them have it.

We were told before hand that we were going to take over a Jewish cemetery to protect the 3rd Battalion's flank. We started out and everybody was happy-go-lucky, because we didn't anticipate any fighting on this trip. We'd gotten a good way down in the field and Shelps, with two other guys, were walking in a triangle close together.

I yelled to them, "Shelps, don't bunch up like that. The Germans will throw a mortar right in on you, buddy."

He replied, "Aw, the hell with the Germans," and no sooner than he had gotten this out of his mouth, a mortar shell fell in between them and got all three. I don't know whether it killed them or not, but we didn't let that deter us. We kept on going! As we advanced closer to the Germans, they were shooting mortars at us. I don't know how many machine guns, but they were raking the open field and our guys were dropping like flies.

There was a battalion lieutenant up ahead of me, and one of those machine gun bullets hit him in the spine, and to my dying day I'll be able to hear the scream that poor man gave. It is indescribable! It made your blood curdle. There were so many being killed and wounded that it demoralized the whole battalion. We saw this sloped canal bank and, that being the only cover available, ran for the protection it afforded, got there and laid down flat. We thought we were out of their sight, but those Germans were pretty smart. They moved their machine guns along that sloped bank and started shooting down the bank. While they didn't get me, they got a few of the guys. You could hear them falling over into the water. All of us yelled, "Heck, this ain't no good." We started running towards the rear, retreating. Officer Collen was up there with us, and he was still out in the field. He wouldn't get out. I don't know! That guy could not be hit.

He pulled off his helmet, raised his hands over his head, and said, "Hey, you men, we're not retreating. We're going on in and get those Kraut son-of-a-bitches. Come on with me, and help me. We're going to get them!" Everybody reluctantly stopped, and we slowly started following him, but I think he realized the odds were against us. We advanced up the field and saw this mound of old red dirt — I don't know why it was there. It was pretty big and we hadn't seen it before. I guess it was too far away. We finally made it and had protection from the machine guns.

The Germans began to shell us and Officer Collen got on the phone to regiment and he called for smoke; the smoke came. He got back on the phone and he said, "Look, my men have been in combat too long and haven't had a rest since January 22. We've been on the lines day and night, and they are about to rebel. It's reached the point of rebellion. They are exhausted and hungry. We need some damn tanks up here and we need them quick, because we've run into heavy opposition." It wasn't long until we heard the tanks coming. First, a couple of them came and finally we ended up having six or eight, including a TD. Wherever you saw one or two tanks, there was a TD (tank destroyer) with them. The tank destroyer always had the 90 millimeter gun on it. Those tankers, under cover of smoke, came to this mound where we were. We were all hungry and the tankers began getting their rations out and eating. We told them we were hungry, and this one tanker said, "I'll give you what chow I've got." All he had for me was a can of vegetable stew, which is the worst meal in "C" rations. I couldn't eat much of it, because we couldn't heat it up due to the ferocity of battle. He gave me three "D" bars — concentrated chocolate. One of these was supposed to last a whole day, but I ate two of them, I was so hungry I then became sick and vomited, finally getting it out of my system.

To this day, as my wife will attest, I never have eaten much chocolate. It's only been in most recent years that I have eaten it. If I eat any chocolate at Christmas, it has to be with cream or coconut filling; no chocolate cake. Hot chocolate was out of the question. I couldn't drink it because of the horrible taste from being sick, as a result of overeating the rich "D" bars.

They kept replenishing the smoke which hid us from the Krauts, causing them to quit shooting. About four or five o'clock the next morning, we were told to get on the tanks. We were going to go in and knock out the enemy machine guns. Everybody climbed on the tanks. There were only a few of us left, due to high casualties. I was the last one to get on and had to get on the tail end of the tank, holding onto another comrade. We moved out slowly toward the Krauts. There were three tanks abreast. I was riding the middle tank. We had a tank destroyer following us. A German tank at our right front, near the edge of town opened fire on us and missed. When he fired, the tank destroyer responded with several rounds, knocking the enemy tank out. We had no more problems with the Kraut tanks.

Aboard our tanks, we advanced towards their machine guns. Would you believe those silly Germans opened up on us with machine gun fire, and when they did my tank stopped and fired three rapid shots with the 75 millimeter shell. The noise from the big gun's blast was deafening. My ears were ringing, and I almost fell off the tank. The adrenaline of everyone was sky high; we wanted revenge. I had been promoted to squad leader and was off the tank first yelling for my men to follow, and get the Kraut bastards. My squad needed no further words. They reacted splendidly and came after me. I spotted an enemy machine gun nest and headed straight for it. I went for the gunner, who with his two helpers, had their helmets off and their hands raised. I reached over the machine gun, grabbed him by the hair and with my left hand, jerked him out of the foxhole over the machine gun. He was real small and frightened to the point, he was trembling. I searched him, got his watch and a P—38 gun, while two of my men performed the same act with his helpers. We rounded up all the machine gunners and riflemen, searched them, and made them get in a group with their hands clasped behind their heads. By daybreak, we had cleared the area killing a large number of Germans. The prisoners, in a group, heavily guarded, were marched back to the rear to a Prisoner-of-War cage.

Before we pulled back to regroup, we knew this was a Jewish cemetery. A group of us looked at the names and dates on the tombstones which were very interesting, as I always occasionally visited cemeteries and they seemed to tell a story. This particular one being Jewish was of special interest, as this cemetery was filled with bodies identified with the nationality of Jesus Christ. The dates were old, and the cemetery had trees growing on it; names were very unusual to me as I never met a Jew until I went into the Army. My knowledge of this group of people was confined to what I had read in the Bible. Our casualties were very heavy in this battle, and it was ironic to fight in the home of the dead.

This battle was one of the most unusual and frightening times of my life. While we were at this mound waiting to attack the Germans, replacements came up and several were assigned to my squad. I did not get their names that night, and one of them was killed by enemy shells within five minutes from the time he arrived.

The violent battle on the part of our battalion helped our 3rd Battalion in their battle for Biesheim as they, too, had a severe time securing the town, due to the fanatical group of enemy encountered. They, like us, were outnumbered four to one. Knocking out the pocket on their left flank relieved a lot of pressure. The 1st Battalion of the 15th Regiment passed through us and continued on, which also helped our 3rd Battalion.

We moved back into the little town from where we had jumped off. We could hear the heavy fighting up at Biesheim, where the 3rd Battalion was fighting for their lives. When we got back everybody was so keyed up they couldn't rest. For some reason or another, I went out on my own. I don't know where I went, but passing between two big houses, I stepped out on the street and saw a jeep coming down the road. The captain and his driver in the front seat had a prisoner in the back, with his hands tied behind him. I must have looked awful. The captain stopped the jeep, and said, "Say, soldier, were you in the fight for the cemetery?"

I replied, "Yes, sir, I was."

He asked me how would I like to have the commanding officer of that group, who was so rough on us?

I replied, "Captain, I would love to have him."

He answered, "I got him in the back seat. The son-of-a-bitch won't talk."

I said, "Well, captain, please turn him over to me, and I'll shoot the son-of-a-bitch."

You could see the fear in the German's eyes. He was cowered down. The captain laughed, and said, "No, I'm going to take him back and we will get the information out of the son-of-a-bitch."

I bade him good luck and emphasized, "If you need my help, my name is Craft with C Company and I would love to take care of him."

I went back to the house, where my platoon was staying. Nobody was really resting. We didn't get hot chow, but we were able to, at least, shave and comb our hair and everybody tried to get a haircut. We always had somebody that could cut hair. Finally, we were cleanly shaven and got a little rest and relaxation. This was probably about February 2, 1945. We were able to stay there that night. This was near Biesheim, and I don't know how close to Colmar it was. I do know the 3rd Battalion had taken a beating there, because the houses were booby trapped; they had tiger tanks to face and they really had a fight on their hands. The Germans had booby trapped our wounded.

CHAPTER 16
THE BATTLE OF VOGLESHEIM

Our rest was short-lived. I think at this particular time, the 7th Infantry was the only one that was really fighting the enemy. The 15th and 30th Infantry were off the lines or in defensive positions. On the 5th of February, here again, we were not told where we were going, but were told to move out. We moved out walking on the highway for a long distance. As we got closer to the enemy, we left the road through a muddy field. By that time our artillery had begun to open up, and the rear echelon had designed a new weapon called "artificial moonlight." It was thrown way up high over our heads, pointed in the face of the enemy. This supposedly gave us an advantage. I'm not sure whether it did or not, but at least it was light. As we moved in the field, closer to the lines, the Germans opened up on us with artillery and machine guns. I thought the snow was terrible to compete with, but now we were bogging down knee deep in mud. The thaw had begun with very little snow left. It seems to me the snow had left while we were pulled back resting. The ground had been freshly plowed in the fall. All the water from the snow going into it made it mushy.

A and C Companies were in the most forward elements of the attack. B Company was following, cleaning up what we bypassed. It's very interesting to note that there is a write-up about our company commander, which states: "First Lieutenant Katz, Commanding Company A displayed great leadership during the attack on Vogelsheim. He urged his men forward through the two impact areas of artillery and tank fire. Although, he was wounded four times by shell fragments, he rushed from man to man, while shells exploded close by." Well, I happen to know that he was one of the most cowardly officers that I ever ran across. I don't believe this story. His cowardice could only be second to that of Lieutenant Sauer. I recall my reaction, when I first read this book back in 1946. My notation said, "Who in the world told this story? Katz, the son-of-a-bitch, I bet. Tain't true."

Nevertheless, we continued on across the field, and it almost killed us physically. We finally got back on the highway, just before getting into the town of Vogelsheim, which was our last mission in the Colmar Pocket. We arrived there under heavy fire. Each platoon had an area assigned to them. I don't remember the name of the street assigned to my platoon, and I didn't know it at that time. I could probably go back, if it hasn't changed, and find it. We went down the street, one squad on each side. Being raw recruits, my scouts were afraid. I couldn't get anything out of them. I kept yelling and yelling at them to go on, to knock out windows and locked doors. We couldn't get in — couldn't knock them down — so we knocked out windows and threw grenades in each house. We cleared every house to the end of the street, where it intersected with another street. I looked to the right on the street and saw two tanks.

I was leading my men and thought they were our own. We listened and heard the clanking of metal, and then realized it was the Germans. Not having a bazooka or rifle grenade, I motioned for my men to back up. We got to the corner house and hid. The Germans knew that we were near, because we'd made enough noise. They cranked up the lead tank. Apparently, they'd been hitching a disabled one to it. They backed up, turned it around and came right by us, getting away. They were 10 to 15 feet away, but we didn't want to be dead heroes, since we only had the M-1 rifles. We scouted around, but found no more Germans. I know they were bound to have been bedded up in the cellars, etc. We couldn't find them at night.

It was pitch dark, and the town was burning. The Germans began to shell us. We went back down to report to the platoon sergeant that we'd cleared our area. He said, "Craft, take your men and put up outposts all along this street, which faces a huge field. They will have to be spread thin. When you get that done, report back to me." I got my men together, and again, I was leading the way. We were walking in the center of the street single file, and they were all behind me. We were moving very cautiously, because we knew there were Germans still in town.

Suddenly, I heard German boots clicking on the cobblestone. I motioned my men to stop. It was a German, all right! He came off the sidewalk into the middle of the street. He was coming right towards me, and I could see his figure in the darkness. When he got within about five feet from me, I called out, "Hand aho." He began to say, "I'm an officier and I want to surrender to an officier," and he didn't attempt to raise his hands. I said, "You Kraut son-of-a-bitch, you'd better put your hands up. Macht schnel. Raise your hands, or I will gut shoot you right here." He quickly raised his hands. By that time, I had my gun in his belly. My men behind me got awfully brave by that time. They came up while he had his hands up and began to search him. The first things we searched for were watches and guns. This particular guy had a very good watch, and it was halfway between his wrist and elbow. He did that to conceal it. If he was captured, he had hoped it might be overlooked. We didn't realize what a prize capture we had. One guy got his pistol, one his watch, and I didn't get anything, because I was the one that had my gun on him. I sent one of the boys back with him. He had an attache case in his hand. At the time, I didn't think too much about it, but I heard later that when they carried him back to the company CP, the 1st Sergeant Beeson went through his briefcase and found a very expensive 35 millimeter camera. They also found elaborate defense plans of the Germans. This never was recorded in the history book, but our 1st sergeant found the camera, and the company commander got a hold of him after they saw those plans and made him talk.

What had happened to the prisoner was that he'd been on furlough and had just rejoined his unit, picked up his orders and was briefed. He was a forward artillery observer. That's why he had all those German gun and troop positions marked on the map in his possession. As you can see, he didn't get a chance to destroy the maps, and that gave our side a great break. This was something, which neither I, my squad, my platoon or my company received any recognition for, but that's quite all right. There are a lot of things that happened in combat, where individuals were not recognized, except the people that really were in a position to obtain the awards. They knew how to go about it, and had access to the right people to apply for them.

Anyway, I posted my men, and I went back to check with Sergeant Silks. Before I did, Silks had one fellow with him, and they were on an outpost. I heard a commotion, maybe 50 or 75 feet down the street, near the intersection that D Company was guarding. There was a row of houses next to a wide field, facing the street the first platoon had cleared. In most of these towns, they had pillars up to indicate that you were going into some kind of enclosure. I'm sure it was a false type thing, probably like the thing we have here in Ridgeway Estates, when you come off Ridgeway. Nevertheless, they had a wall going from there to the first house, at least. It was a pretty high wall. You couldn't see over it, and there was a German on the other side. One of the boys from D Company was trying to get him to surrender. The German was talking to him, and he'd begun to shy away. He was trying to lure the GI's over, so they could ambush them. We were too smart for that. He shut up, and we decided to pull back and take cover. There was a heavy machine gun set up in the back door of a house. The back door of the house had steps and a little porch off of the kitchen, but there were a number of steps. It was higher than my head. And, to take protection from the cold, they had set up the machine gun in the doorway. They were all talking, when all of a sudden I heard something coming through the air, or I sensed it, or my intuition told me this.

I had my rifle in my right hand, and I apparently raised my left hand. Some sort of anti-tank gun was shooting at our machine gun in the doorway. At the most, I could only have been five feet away from that machine gun. It hit the machine gun direct and exploded. All kinds of debris fell on me, and killed those three men instantly, knocking the machine gun out. All at once, I realized that my left arm was paralyzed. I didn't have any feeling in it. We were scrambling around and found a basement in the house. All of the GI's were going in it. There was a bunch of them, and I decided that I'd go down and check and see what was going on. I got in there, and we were talking and I said, "I'm not going to let the Krauts catch me in this cellar and murder me.

I want to be where I can have a little protection." I started to walk out the door and a guy walked over and blocked my way and said, "Soldier, I'm a 2nd lieutenant in the United States Army and I order you to stay with us." I replied, "I don't give a damn, if you are a colonel in whose Army. Get out of my way, because I'm not going to stay in this death trap; besides, I've got some of my own men to take care of. I came over to help you guys out." I shoved him out of the way and walked out.

The CP was across the street from there and by that time, I saw a German jeep burning. I went inside and told the medic about my arm. I don't remember his name, but he rubbed my arm with alcohol, rubbed it vigorously for an hour and I still didn't have any feeling in it. After a couple of hours, maybe three, I don't know, the feeling started coming back, and it really hurt. That's where I was told that 1st Sergeant Beeson had found the expensive camera and they had gotten all this information out of the German field observer's attache case. During the conversation, it seems like old Meadows, who was a runner for the CP, was standing on guard by the front door, and a German jeep came down the street. Ironically, he was the driver of the jeep for the field artillery observer, whom I had captured a few hours back. The jeep driver drove down the street, past the CP, and turned around to go back. Meadows recognized it being the enemy, and hollered, "Halt." He didn't stop. Meadows shot and the Kraut driver stopped the jeep, jumped out the other side and ran between the houses back to his lines. He was in such a rush, that he left the engine running, with the lights on, and when we left the town, two or three days later, those lights were still on. He must have had a good battery. The jeep must have run out of gas.

I passed by the jeep, shied away from it, because I didn't know if it was booby trapped or not, and I figured the thing could burn up or run out of gas, or do whatever. I didn't care! I went on back to talk to Sergeant Silks, told him I had all my men on outposts, where I had been, and my experience, and he said, "Go on up there where you can check on them; keep them from going to sleep," which I did.

I had one man who was by himself, a fellow named Sparks, from Chicago. I thought Sparks was all right, even though he was of German descent, as all of this type of people I had come in contact with hated the Germans. We spent the night there. The next day, about mid-morning, we were looking out across this field and there was a company of Germans running towards the town, shooting and, boy, did they look awesome. I'm telling you that they really looked like they were super men. All of us opened up on them. Machine guns, BAR's, and I was shooting a rifle. I know I must have shot half of my ammunition or more. All of a sudden, I looked over there at Sparks, and he had his head down. He was crying! I said, "Sparks, what in the hell is wrong with you? Why aren't you shooting those damn Krauts?"

He replied, "Oh, I can't shoot my own flesh and blood." I said, "Well, you yellow son-of-a-bitch!" I threw my empty gun at him, saying, "Load it, and give me yours," and started shooting his gun. "You keep it loaded. I can shoot them."

We made it too hot for them. I don't know how many we killed, but apparently there was a deep trench in the center of this field, and they ran back and got in the ditch. I don't know which direction they went in. I think they took off to our right. By that time, one of our own field artillery observers came up to question me about the Germans whereabouts and what had happened. I told him about how many yards, which was an estimate; where they jumped in the ditch and disappeared. Then I asked, "Why don't you lay a barrage down there?" He was kind of skeptical. He never did order the artillery, but that afternoon, February 5, 1945, the 30th Infantry came through us, and they were going to take the Neuf-Brisach area. That was supposed to have been a mighty fortress, but I understand that they didn't really have to fight for it, as the artillery did a good shelling job with their gun and troop emplacements due to the information revealed from the briefcase of the German artillery observer that I had captured earlier. There was a little bit of confusion, because of their going through us. We were happy to see that somebody was between us and the Germans.

Along about mid-afternoon, after they'd gone through us, it was decided that there was no need for us to pull heavy guard. Our platoon posted two men at a time on two houses in our area, and they were walking leisurely around. There was an old boy named Rhea, who came from Boston — B A H S T O N — as he called it, and the French Morrocans began to bring prisoners into our area. The house that we occupied had a courtyard with a high wrought iron fence. It must have been 10 or 12 feet high. There were brick walls four or five feet high, with wrought iron built into the top. It was very pretty. This must have been an expensive home. The Ghoums came up and said that they had a lot of prisoners. They wanted to know if they could put them in the enclosed area, where it could be locked, so that they couldn't get away, and they wouldn't have to be guarded so closely. We said, "Sure." Ole Rhea and I were fooling around out behind the house, looking for chickens and rabbits, and we found about six or eight rabbits. We were talking and smoking. A German prisoner came up to the locked gate behind the bars, and wanted to know if he could have a cigarette, speaking perfect English. We told him, "Sure," and we gave him one. Rhea and I were anxious to know how things were going back in Germany. We apparently got the wrong guy. He was a true Nazi. Rhea and I would take turns in talking to him. He said to us, "I don't understand! Both of you are Americans, yet you don't talk alike." Rhea explained to him that he was from B A H S T O N, and I was from Mississippi. The German still didn't know how to react to our different accents. We tried to get chummy with him in order to get some information by asking him how things were going in Germany. We told him the war was about over; that the Germans were licked, and he said, "No" that wasn't the case, that morale in Germany was still very high. Germany hadn't been touched by bombs. They'd been able to drive our aircraft away, and the German Air Force was tearing England up. He said the Germans were going to let us get to Germany, and then they were going to counter—attack, then push us back into the channel. We laughed at him and told him what he already knew, that Germany was whipped the second time, and he walked away.

We proceeded to take an inventory of rabbits again. We couldn't find any chickens or eggs. None of the men knew how to fry rabbits. I told them, "You kill and skin them." They didn't know how, and I showed them. We found some cooking grease, flour, salt and pepper and I put those rabbits on and country fried the meat. I had to do a lot of the skinning of the rabbits, too. It made me sick and I didn't want the doggone rabbits. I'm telling you, they thought the rabbit was delicious. It was hot and good meat, because they were big white rabbits. The boys thoroughly enjoyed the meal.

The next day, we were told that we were moving out, and to get ready. Trucks were waiting up about a half mile down the road out of town. For some reason, the trucks didn't want to come into town. We got in battalion formation, and walked to the trucks, getting into them. It took a lot of time to get everybody situated. By then, it was nearly noon. I was on the rear truck of the convoy, and all of a sudden, out of nowhere, a German plane appeared. We jumped out, and began shooting at him with our rifles, along with the ack—ack guns, but the son-of-a-bitch managed to slip in and drop the bomb. It couldn't have been too big of a bomb, but it knocked several houses down. That got the drivers on those trucks real busy. The plane took off, after he dropped the one bomb — it was just a hit and run situation, but in doing this the pilot was very bold.

CHAPTER 17
SECOND WATCH ON THE RHINE

During this campaign, I lost many dear friends, including Sergeant White and Johnny Clayton, both wounded. My friend, Traim, who started with the division in Africa, was killed during the ambush at the Chateau. Many other of my friends were killed, captured or wounded. Now it was replacements I had to lead.

The convoy began to move out shortly after that, taking us back to the German prisoner-of-war camp, where we arrived on February 8, 1945. It was on the Rhine River and was located near the place where we had so much trouble in the Jewish cemetery. It was right across the canal from the cemetery and on the bank of the Rhine River. We had to pull guard on the river in foxholes. Being squad leader, I'd been promoted to buck sergeant, and I didn't have to pull guard. All I had to do was designate who pulled guard in my squad. I don't know how long we stayed there, but I do know that we were so exposed, that they brought in the smoke machines and pumped smoke to keep the Germans from seeing us. We didn't actually pull any patrols across the Rhine River. That was something I missed out on, since I got to stay back in the German barracks, play cards and shoot the bull. We stayed there for several days. The Germans would come across in a boat, and they'd catch our guys in the foxholes asleep, and take them as prisoner, or slit their throats, then go back across the river. This happened on several occasions. You always had folks going to sleep on their outpost. I was always thankful that the good Lord was always with me, because that never happened to me.

Before we pulled out of Vogelsheim, General Grafton came down in his jeep. He was driving along the road congratulating all of us for a job well done. We then stayed at this German concentration camp until February 18, 1945, when we were relieved by the Ghoums. Then we moved back to Belleville, north of Nancy, France, to regroup and take the river crossing. We knew what that meant. That meant to cross the Rhine River. We didn't know the Seigfried Line was still in front of us. For our performance in the Colmar Pocket, at a colorful ceremony, the 3rd Division was awarded the French Fourragere by the French Government, headed by General DeGaulle. We were always quite proud of that, because this was one of the bloodiest battles of the war, which was never publicized. People in the States never did know about it. It happened at the same time, or shortly after the Battle of the Bulge; that being where all the publicity went. It seemed like the 7th Army never got publicity. I don't know whether it was their public relations or what, but that's the way it was. We couldn't change that and did not care.

In the battle for Vogelsheim, the Germans really shelled us. I knew of one GI that was killed when one of those shells hit the house he was in. He didn't have a scratch on him, but it killed him. He died of a concussion. We lost a lot of men in the capture of the town of Vogelsheim, but I didn't get a scratch, other than a contusion in my left arm.

We'd gotten a pretty good rest, except we had to be on constant guard, trying to keep the Germans from crossing the Rhine River in force. After getting back to Belleville, France, we had a good time. Actually, we were oriented on river crossings. When we got back there, we pulled a few exercises on how to go and take machine guns, and were given information on how to cross the river — that type of thing. Then, things began to get a little secretive. They ordered us to turn in all of our helmets, for removal of the division insignia. Furthermore, we were told to take all shoulder patches off, so we could not be identified, if captured by the enemy. We knew from this that there was something pretty big coming. All the vehicles had been repainted, removing all insignias, and unit insignias from all equipment and from us, personally. Although, we were sweating out the crossing of the Rhine River, we had a good time from February 18 to March 13, 1945.

One day, they had a decorations day and the whole division lined up. We went by truck to a large field for a parade and an awards ceremony. They had built platforms, etc. I was one of the participants in the decorations. I had gotten a Purple Heart for being hit in the back. There were various medals awarded and General Patch, being the Commanding Officer of the 7th Army, was there. I walked up onto the platform and saluted him. He returned the salute. Then he pinned the Purple Heart on me. They mailed the original Purple Heart back to my parents. At that time in Belleville, France, I often thought of my mother and father, and my brother, because I was concerned about him getting into the mess I was in. Other than that, I didn't think too much about the people back home. I didn't have time. Our main objective, it seemed, was to stay alive and get something hot to eat, be able to wash our feet and face, and get somebody to trim our hair; it was growing so long. Clean clothes were a luxury.

They took the combat shoe packs off of us, which were rubberized up to slightly below our ankle. It was leather from there up and they were good; they didn't leak. They made your feet sweat, and they were damp all the time. That's what made our feet susceptible to frostbite during the bitter cold. There were times that I longed to get frost bitten feet. One time, I bathed my feet in snow. Maybe that had something to do with why I didn't get frost-bitten feet. We had not had a change of clothes in three months; neither had we had a bath. I don't recall having a hot meal during this period of time. To be behind the lines with hot chow, clean clothes and a house for shelter was living in luxury.

One night, I dreamed about my grandmother, Florence Craft. She used to tell me stories about the Civil War and how her uncle, Bob Hester, and a cousin of hers had fought in the Civil War and were wounded. What terrible hardships they had to undergo. She said to me, "Well, son, you know I told you those stories about the Civil War about my Uncle Bob and my cousin; I never thought, that when I was telling you the stories, that you'd be here in a similar situation." I woke up and that disturbed me quite a bit. It took several days to shake it off.

This time we had to pull speed marches and take training. I got replacements which made a full squad. Among them were two young men who had taken their basic training together. Their names were Draughn and Galahad. I made them first and second scouts. While training, these two boys always went out too far from me, where I couldn't keep contact with them. I told them time after time, "Now, boys, look, when we get in combat, it's going to be a different situation. Unless I tell you to, stay in my sight all the time, where I can give you a signal, where I can call out to you." It went in one ear and out the other. Those boys paid no attention to me. When we got in combat, they did the same thing. Because of this, Draughn went out once, and was probably shot accidentally by his squad leader. By that time, I had gotten promoted to platoon guide, and was a staff sergeant.

During our stay at Belleville, we did not train too vigorously, and we were allowed passes to go to the city of Nancy, France. A friend of mine, along with several other members of our company got a pass, also. We paired off on the highway, thumbed a jeep, and hitched a ride to Nancy. We began to enjoy the sights there and went into a pastry shop. GI's always had their money in large denominations, and the French merchants couldn't change it. You gave him a large bill, and you'd have a pocket full of paper money and all kinds of little coins. We didn't want much pastry, just something sweet to eat. We purchased donuts and some kind of coffee cake. I was trying to pay the Frenchman. He didn't have any change. I had my money in my hand, and I could not understand French. I gave him a 100 Franc note, and he could not make change. I understood this and pulled out a handful of coins, but was not making any progress, as we did not understand each other.

A sweet feminine voice spoke in perfect English, saying, "Soldier, you have the correct change in your hand." She reached in my hand and got the coin and gave it to him and said, "That's what he wants." I said, "Well, fine!" I was stunned momentarily and before I could say "Thank you," she turned and walked out of the shop. I wanted to talk to the young lady, because I hadn't heard an English speaking female voice in a long time. It was very pleasant to hear one again. Before I could pursue her, she had disappeared into the crowd.

We looked Nancy over the rest of the day, and went to a restaurant for something to eat. I didn't enjoy French coffee, neither did I enjoy their cooking. It was the fact that we were free to do it without fear of being shot at that made it so enjoyable. Along about 4:00 or 5:00 o'clock in the afternoon, we approached a truck driver, who knew exactly where we were billeted. He carried us home. We used to talk and reminiscence about home and various battles. Sergeant Silks was always bucking for a higher rank. He got a battlefield promotion to go to Officers Candidate School. Greene was promoted to platoon sergeant, and I was promoted to platoon guide. We stayed there throughout the time, did a little training and were oriented about a special secret mission. We were going to attack the Germans from a different territory, or sector. We were read the articles of war. We were told that if we were captured, to give our name, rank and serial number. I don't know if you could get away with that with the enemy or not. They could obtain information from you, if they so minded, by using various torture techniques.

All this happened from February 19, 1945, to March 13, 1945. While taking the river crossing training, we were billeted out several nights in tents, which must have held 50 to 100 men. One night, I didn't have anything to do and was at the far end talking to some of the boys in the platoon. Being one of the older guys, they were always trying to pick me for information. My position of platoon guide made me look real high in their eyes. They didn't know I wasn't any better off than they were! The only advantage it gave me is that I didn't have to pull as much guard duty. I could designate someone else to do it.

While we were talking, there was a voice from the other end of the tent saying, "Does anybody know where Sergeant William B. Craft is?" When I heard the voice, I knew who it was. I said, "Hell, yeah, Buford Lowery, come on in!" He came on back to where I was and we started talking. For privacy purposes, we left the tent and went off by ourselves talking about the war and back home until two or three o'clock in the morning. We had a very good time. Being able to talk to a dear friend from Smith County was a shot in the arm for both of us and to learn that Buford was okay. This was the last time I saw him, until after I returned home.

We were put on trucks and carried back toward the front lines headed for Germany. We put the regular all leather combat boots on. My left boot badly pinched the area around my ankle. Apparently, my feet and ankles had spread out due to the flexibility of the rubber boot. This gave me serious trouble until late March, as I experienced difficulty in walking.

CHAPTER 18
INTO GERMANY AND CRACKING THE SIEGFRIED LINE

In spite of the secrecy the division attempted, the Germans were not fooled, because they knew who the 3rd Division was, and I wouldn't be a bit surprised, because reflecting back, they made the initial landing in Africa. They fought all the way through that country, Sicily, made the invasions of Italy at Anzio and took Rome, assisted in the capture of Rome, and then went on to make the invasion of Southern France. They were in continuous combat from the invasion of Southern France up until November 19th, the time we had about a week off, before the crossing of the Meurthe River. The 15th Regiment stayed on the front lines with the Germans. The Germans certainly had information about our division. There's no doubt in my mind, that we gave them a lot of trouble. I was plagued with this combat boot, pinching my left ankle and had to limp a little. Moving on up by truck during the night of the 13th or 14th of March, 1945, we went through Pompey, Nancy, on Highway Number 74, and then there were other towns called Mayenvic Diluze, Fenetrange, Sara-Union, Oerhinger, and Kalhausen we went through to assembly areas in the vicinity of Singling, France. The regiment made a 75 mile motor march without incident and was closed in the new area at 2:30, 0230 o'clock.

Reconnaissance was conducted and plans formulated for the new offensive plan. These trucks did not take us all the way. They couldn't go on the front lines, and I recall the first incident — we were some few miles behind the front, and the whole regiment was marching towards it; we went in single file on each side of the highway. About mid-afternoon, as I recall, we were walking along, and all of a sudden six German fighters appeared in the sky and they made one sweep at us, firing their machine guns — they were strafing us.

We saw them, knew we were sitting ducks and headed for the field, scattered and fell down in the prone position. They were making a hit and run because one plane was able to make a run with his machine guns. He made this one sweep, and it seemed as if he had a whip. Those bullets were acting like a whip when you throw it, and they were hitting the highway where we'd been. Our anti-aircraft guns started shooting, making it so hot for them, that they had to turn tail and head back towards Germany.

I didn't hear of any casualties. I didn't see any. However, you have to understand a regiment was a large group of men. With that many men, you can't possibly know everything that is going on. Our primary interest was self preservation. I knew that I wasn't injured, nor any of the people in my immediate vicinity. As soon as the plane was chased off, we got back on the road and started to march. I don't recall the instances where we stopped. Apparently, we must have reached our destination, because we did go through the 44th Infantry Division. The enlisted men were not given any instructions. Apparently, the 44th Infantry Division had not been giving the Germans too much trouble; the Germans hadn't been giving them a lot, either, because the Krauts had been able to put up an elaborate defense, especially with regard to mine fields. They laid a lot of mines. It was a difficult thing to get through the mine fields, since they had a physiological effect on you. Once you were in one of them, you didn't know if you were going to be able to get out or not. Our artillery performed beautifully that morning as they laid down a heavy barrage on the enemy stronghold.

We pushed off at 0100 on the morning of March 15, 1945. Immediately after we got through the 44th Infantry Division, and on our way to Germany, the engineer battalion set up search lights that went over our heads. Artificial moonlight, they called it, because practically all of our fighting was done at night, and had been for some time back since the Colmar Pocket. We walked and walked. I was a platoon guide, and was at the rear of the platoon. A platoon guide's job is keeping people intact, and not falling by the wayside.

We had men that were soft. We had them from the Air Corps, artillery, and from all branches of the service, because infantry men were getting very low at this time. We walked that morning, and Sparks, the German who couldn't kill his own blood brothers, was made a rifleman. But he carried extra ammunition for the grenadier. We were expecting a lot of tanks. Sparks would slow down. He'd want to drag back and get behind me. I kept on and on after him. He said, "This is heavy." So, in spite of his attitude about not being able to kill the enemy, I was a little sympathetic, and even though I pressed him to go on, he seemed to be tired out. I started carrying his ammunition for him. He would still linger back and not keep up. I kept after him, and finally, he didn't want to keep up with me carrying his ammunition for him, which was heavy. I told him, "By golly, if you can't keep up like everybody else, you can carry the ammunition yourself. I'm not carrying it any more."

When we got into the first fire fight, that's the last I saw or heard of Sparks. Apparently, he took off. We had a great big guy named Bonner from Massachusetts out of the Air Corps. He must have been six feet, six inches tall and probably weighed 225 pounds. He was having difficulty, and I carried his rifle and some things he had, to relieve him. In fact, I carried things for everybody to help them out, because even though I was very small in stature, not very heavy, I really had endurance. We had a few fights and we went over some big hills, etc., with the Germans shooting at us. They were throwing artillery, but didn't do much damage to us. Certainly, they had us on our toes. That type of thing was really frightening.

Along about daybreak, our final objective was to take a hill, that was a wooded area. We had a small arms fire fight. It was in the spring and rather foggy. I don't know whether it was from the gun smoke or fog, or it might have been a combination of both, but we got on the hill that the Charlie Company was assigned to take. We took it without incident. It was out from a small village. I don't recall the name. We were all on our toes. Across the valley, sometime during the day, we looked up and there appeared to be a company, or a battalion, of Germans coming our way. We could see them. They knew where we were, but there was a big tiger tank down in the valley. He'd been shelling us. The shelling we took was demoralizing, but the German tank saw this group of his own men coming in formation to surrender. I don't know whether he had radio contact with them or not, most certainly he did, but they didn't stop. He started shelling his own men. They scattered and I don't know what happened to them. I know from the mood they were in, they were willing to surrender. We directed artillery fire on the tank, and eventually got him. Sometime during the mid-afternoon, we thought we had our area protected. I guess we got careless, because we were tired. When you are looking at a situation like this, someone did get careless, because a lone German infiltrated our positions. He got behind a tree in between two fellows and shot one in the back of the head. No sooner than he shot the GI, than the GI on the other side of the German killed him. I've often wondered about that. There were two dead people, and had this German come up and surrendered, we would have gladly taken him as a prisoner. He chose the other route and got one of us, and we got him. But there were no further incidents on this hill.

We didn't stay there too long. We were moving out in the attack again. I don't want to forget this bit of information that happened to my good buddy Buford Lowery. Buford was in the 2nd Battalion of the 7th Infantry. Unlike us, they really encountered the mine fields. This was near Utwiler, Germany. I don't think that our company was the first troops in Germany, but a boy from B Company, 7th Infantry was the first one of the 3rd Division to step across the line. The 2nd Battalion moved out into the attack, and they hadn't gone but a short way when they hit this elaborate defense of mine fields. As soon as the mines began to explode the Germans were alerted and to make matters worse they started throwing in their artillery on the 2nd Battalion. It was dark! There was confusion, and I understand from Buford that they didn't have a radio. Something had happened to it. It got knocked out or hadn't gotten there. They recouped from this mine field situation in spite of the heavy shelling and the mines, and they went on and took the town of Utwiler. This was apparently the whole battalion. They captured the town with a lot of prisoners. This is the way the Germans usually reacted. They would retreat and then they would counter-attack. In this counter-attack, they had tiger tanks and there was no way of stopping them, unless you got behind them with a bazooka team. The Germans retreated, and they came back into the town. They were not only shelling it with tanks, but artillery and mortars. The 2nd Battalion had to find shelter. They were defenseless, and poor Buford, along with some more of his immediate squad or platoon, got into a cellar. The Germans knocked the building down on them and then threw grenades through the windows on them, and Buford got hit with a fragment of a grenade.

The Germans gave them a chance to come out and surrender. Buford and his buddies, through necessity, surrendered. Their battalion commander was almost captured. He, his runner, and maybe another officer or two, ran, got in a bomb crater that was filled with water, and they hid in it. Perhaps that's the reason that they were not captured. I understand there was a stray sergeant who ran out of this place and reached the elements of the 30th Infantry Regiment, reporting to them what had happened. They didn't have any contact with the 2nd Battalion. They got the report, that they had been wiped out. The 30th Regiment Headquarters notified the 7th Regiment Headquarters and the 3rd Battalion went to their rescue. Companies 1 and L, were reinforced with the anti-tank guns and the 10th Artillery Battalion was instructed to put a heavy concentration of fire on Utwiler, and the surrounding area. It was really an act of revenge, because they poured in a heavy barrage. Companies 1 and L went on in and knocked out the tanks and German equipment, recapturing the town. There were very few of those GI's that came out of this alive. There were nine officers, and 175 enlisted men left out of the 2nd Battalion.

In Company E, there was one officer and 10 enlisted men that escaped. This was Buford Lowery's company. He was taken prisoner-of-war. In Company F, two enlisted men. In Company G, one officer and 39 enlisted men. In Company H, three officers and 68 enlisted men. The Krauts even got the Battalion Headquarters, because there were only four officers and 56 enlisted men left. There was a total of 184 men left in the 2nd Battalion.

That same night we went out into the attack again. Apparently, our objective was Mendelshein, and we walked and walked and walked. I'll never know how many miles. Coming into the small village of Mendelshein, we encountered some German resistance. As usual, we were taking constant shelling, harassing, and deliberate fire. If you will recall, I mentioned two replacements back in Belleville, France, where we had received a lot of replacements, and two of these young men were Draughn and Galahad. I was a squad leader when they joined our platoon; they were in my squad. These two young men were fine young fellows and they were eager to get the

Germans. It was a strange thing about them. They seemed to know a lot of the answers. In fact, they thought that they knew all the answers, and I had cautioned them about getting too far ahead of their squad leader; that they should always look to him for directions. Even while we were talking, they didn't seem to pay a lot of attention. They didn't understand. I'll never be able to comprehend this. I was promoted up to a platoon guide. We make Bulin a buck sergeant, and they were in his squad. When we encountered this resistance in Mendelshein, Draughn got too far out. We were in a fire fight and in a wooded area outside of the town, and the underbrush was heavy. Galahad always thought that Bulin was the one that shot Draughn. If he did, it was not intentional. It was a horrible mistake. I always felt badly about this. I had cautioned those boys and cautioned them about getting too far ahead. Even after I wasn't their squad leader, I talked to them. It didn't seem to ring a bell. Galahad always had a little animosity toward Bulin.

We went on and took the town. We went all the way through this little village. I don't know exactly how they operated. There were a number of houses, I don't know whether there were 100 or 200 houses. It was comparatively small. We pushed on through it, got to the outer edge and stopped. The Germans knew where we were. They were shelling us. By that time it was getting daybreak, and we commandeered a house. Old Burney, the guy that really liked to loot, seemed to come up with a lot of things. He found this long barn with a screen on it. Burney was up there with four or five guys in the barn. They were trying to milk a cow. They were city boys, and they didn't know how to milk her. They had the cow so upset, she was kicking at them. I heard the commotion and asked them, "What in the world are you all doing?" They said, "We can't milk this cow. She hasn't got any milk." I looked at the bag and said, "She's got plenty of milk." They asked me how I knew, and I replied, "Well, look at her bag. You just don't know how to do it." They said, "Can you milk her?" I said, "Sure, I can milk her. Give me your canteen cup." I walked up to the old cow and started talking to her, patted her on her hips, and pushed her a little bit in a certain spot, where you are supposed to, and it will cause them to back one hind leg up. When I did this, she did exactly that; I knew I was at home! I got a canteen cup and began to milk her. The milk was really flowing, filling the cup fast. I handed it to him, and thought he was going to hold it for me, and old Burney turned the cup up to his lips, and drank it down, foam and all. I said, "Good, gosh, Burney, are you crazy? You are supposed to strain the milk." "Oh, I don't need it strained. It's good like it is." I said, "Well, that's not the way you do it." They wanted some more, and every one of them gave me their steel helmets, and I filled several steel helmets full of milk for them, and they had enough milk.

Somewhere during our attack into Germany, I had gotten a pair of nice field glasses from an artillery officer. They were very good glasses, and we were looking out across a long wide field. We didn't know the extent of it, because we could only see the hill. But after you went down into the valley, and over the hill, it extended a long way. We were watching a German outpost on that hill, and we could see some movement. We were trying to shoot with our rifles. It was far off, and I don't think we ever accomplished anything. I don't know whether we found out if anything was there or not, or whether it was our imagination.

About noon it was decided that we were going out into the attack and go right straight across the field. This was the 1st Battalion. At that time Greene had gone back to the rest camp, and I was acting as the platoon sergeant. We were told that there was a triangle of towns, one on the left of the field, the 45th Division was going to take. The one on the right, our own 3rd Battalion was going to take. The 3rd Battalion had taken theirs by the time we got out in the field, but the 45th Division hadn't shown up for the one on the left. We got down to the center of the field and went down the valley, over the hill, and as soon as we got to the top of the hill the Germans began to open up with machine guns, mortars and artillery. The only thing that we knew to do was to keep on going toward the town. We were having a lot of casualties.

I saw this young man, whom I was quite fond of, and he was either Spanish or Mexican descent. He was a very short guy named Allen Joe. He had a smoke grenade in his right field jacket pocket. We were going in for attack and had our rifles in front of us. A German bullet went through his hand, the stock, his hand and went into his chest pocket. It must have been on his right side, striking the smoke grenade and setting it afire.

I saw poor Allen Joe running like a rabbit in circles, leaping high in the air, screaming. He was on fire. I couldn't stop, because I was in charge of the platoon. I had to keep going, urging the men to keep going. Everybody simultaneously, I don't think an order was given, started running toward the enemy, yelling like mad men. We ran, shooting from the hip, towards the town on our left, which should have been taken by the 45th Division. As we approached the town, there were trees outside of it. Seeing a movement behind one of those trees, I began to shoot at it. I had a tommy gun. I'd shoot at him on one side, and he would dart to the other side. It was a large tree with a big trunk. I yelled for some of the men on the left to shoot at him, and they did. I kept advancing towards him. He had wires in each hand near a battery. Before we got to the trees, it seemed like the earth was exploding underneath us, and smoke was oozing from the ground. He was setting off some sort of charges or mines under our feet. That made me furious, and I was in direct line with the tree. One GI ran right up to him and emptied a tommy gun in him, which had 30 bullets, and everybody that came behind him did the same thing. We were angry and eager to kill any German in sight.

We went into the town, and we came to a wall we could see over. I detected a movement in one of the houses, and hollered for the bazooka man to come up. He did and he was very nervous. He was a young recruit. I told him which house to shoot in, and he swung around and shot at it. When he shot at it, I was facing the back of this bazooka, which was about six inches from me. He shot! The back blast knocked me down and shook me bodily. It damaged my eyes, and I couldn't see. I had shot up all of my ammunition, and so had everybody else. We pulled out of this town, went back into the field for a draw for cover. We couldn't go on and take our objective, because we didn't have any ammunition left. We stayed the rest of the afternoon, and when nightfall came, the officers had gotten their orders by radio. We began to march, and I don't know the direction we were in, but there were trucks awaiting us. We got on them, and we went into town.

We arrived in a town. Apparently, they must have shifted us to a different sector, because it seemed like the division commander had gotten orders for the 3rd Division to attack the Siegfried Line about 3000 yards from where we were. The trucks carried us to some town or village that I didn't even know the name of, and we spent the night there.

I got up the next day, and my foot was bothering me because of that combat boot pinching my ankle, and my eyes were red as fire. I had powder burns around my eyes and on my face from the bazooka blast. The lieutenant said that I ought to go down to the Aid Station and get my eyes checked. I told him that I had a foot problem, too. I took his advice and explained this to the same doctor that never seemed to have much sympathy for me, due to his action on my thumb and back wound. He looked at my eyes, not using any instrument, saying that they were all right. He gave me some medicine to apply to them, and he checked my foot. He asked me where it hurt. I pulled my boot off and showed him. He didn't seem to think that it was necessary that anything be done about it. He didn't even tape it up. I got some tape and taped it myself. I went back and reported what the doctor had said about my eyes. When I told them what he said about my foot, they were disgusted because they knew that I wasn't goldbricking. I believe, if my memory serves me right, we stayed at this place that day, and then we weren't even briefed. In fact, the Siegfried Line had occurred to me, but I didn't realize that we were right on it, or that that was our next objective. Neither did anyone else. Especially the enlisted men.

I was still acting as a platoon sergeant, and sometime about 10 or 11 o'clock that night, (it must have been on the 17th of March 1945), we got on the trucks again and we were carried a good distance, put out, and then we had to walk. We reached our destination just before daybreak, and we were at the edge of a forest. We looked out and saw numerous pill boxes. They looked ghostly. It suddenly dawned on me. I knew then where we were going. I had had a suspicion before that we were near the Siegfried Line, because every now and then we'd run upon a pill box, but the pill boxes that we'd run into between the 15th Infantry those three days were really insignificant, because they could be bypassed or surrounded, and we'd get them. But this situation was a different ball game.

We had no idea that we were going into the main Siegfried Line and were going to take these pill boxes. We hadn't discussed any strategy on how we were going to react, or what our purpose was. We knew that we were going to attack the Germans. All at once, our artillery opened up and laid a heavy barrage down. We noticed a lot of those shells were exploding just before they hit the ground. I was told later that was the type of shell that was used to clear land mines. I suppose that's true, because it seemed to be their strategy. However, the artillery barrage was so severe, the Germans in the first row of pill boxes closed up, and we walked right on by. We didn't know what was up, but just walked between them. They weren't really close together, but were staggered in rows and you could tell it was a very good defense. We went through them, down a hill. A herd of cows were grazing, in spite of all the artillery and shooting. The cows wouldn't move out of our way. We opened up on the cows, killing a few of them. We got to the bottom of the hill, and we had to cross over a huge ditch that was a tank trap. They called it the Dragon's Teeth. They had concrete built up in little pyramids, that dotted an area in front of this ditch. The tanks couldn't maneuver across it. We couldn't get through it. We had to climb down the ditch and climb out of it. After climbing out of it, we started up the other hill, and there was another row of pill boxes. Unknown to us, all these pill boxes were connected by trenches, and they had communication, too, radio and telephones. They knew where we were, and we knew where they were in the pill boxes, but we couldn't do anything about it. We got started up the hill, and they pinned us down. We would shoot at the pill boxes with our M-1's, but that's all we could do. The Germans called their artillery in. They were shooting, shelling us with their 88's, mortars, and they were shooting direct with the 88's from the pill boxes, too. The pill boxes were elaborate defenses. They could house a lot of men. I had heard anywhere from a company to a battalion. I don't know if that's true or not, but they were huge and they were all underground. And around them, they had mines with concertina wire around them. They were placed where there wasn't any way you could slip up on them.

They pinned us down, and they kept shooting at us. There was one little technical sergeant or corporal whose name I can't recall, but he was a new replacement. We had dug foxholes to keep away from the bullets and the 88's, if we could. There was a German sniper that was shooting at us. The machine guns were shooting over us, but they couldn't hit us. But this sniper began to get his toll, and this boy had his foxhole dug and was sitting up, leaning against the edge with his left arm stuck out over the left side. This

German sniper shot this GI through the left elbow, and that kind of word got around. By that time, we began to realize where we were, and we knew that things were rough and frankly, I doubted that we were going to get out of there. We stayed that night in the foxholes, and we didn't have any chow. We had called for smoke to come in and protect us, and that prevented the Germans from seeing us.

The next morning we moved up out of those foxholes, and found a connecting trench to the pill boxes. We all got up to the trench, and a German came running down over the hill. He must have been lost, and we captured him. We had him in the trench with us, and disarmed him. By that time, I had gotten wise to everything, as did Lieutenant Sauer, the same guy I have been referring to all along as a brave lieutenant. Next to him was Lieutenant Katz, and they had their radio with them. They weren't divulging anything to anybody. I had told those guys to pass the word down the line for them to follow me, wherever they went; that I was going to watch Sauer and Katz, and wherever they went, I was going, because I knew that they were going to find some place of safety. Sauer and Katz and the runner got up and took off. I punched the guy next to me, who was Pete, and told him to tell them to follow me. Sauer and Katz made it back to the former foxhole. The Germans were still shelling like mad. This was the beginning of the second day. The whole area was covered with smoke. Then Sauer and their runner jumped up, and started running off to our left. I told Pete, "Let's follow them. They have found something." We did, and you couldn't see anything in all of the artificial smoke; we went by this pill box. It had a dugout place behind it. It was soft dirt. Pete and I hit it, and I kind of slipped and he slipped and fell all the way down. He said, "Hey, Craft, this is a pill box down here." I immediately slid down with him. We found a pill box that was full of GI's, including Katz. I didn't see Sauer, and I don't remember seeing the runner or the radio man. We were sitting in that pill box waiting, trying to await for news.

The Germans were still shelling, and I wondered what had happened to my men. It seems that they either didn't believe what I said (they were all practically new men), or they got their signals mixed up. The story related to me by Bannon from New York, was that Sauer had gotten lost. He went back up to the trench. It was terrific! They were shelling us with heavy stuff. I don't know whether it was heavy mortar similar to our 4.2. It was so terrible that some, including myself, thought it might have been a railroad gun, because the earth would shudder when it would explode.

There were two good fellows, named Harpe and Thornton, who were sitting in the trench. This big shell hit on the edge of the trench, and it caved in, burying three of those guys alive. I didn't know who the other fellow was, but I did know Harpe and Thornton. They tried to dig them out with their hands, but they failed to do so. The men suffocated! Lieutenant Sauer became so demoralized he cried, and he gave the boys a talk in the trench and said, "Now, please don't you dare call me lieutenant. You call me Bill." He took his lieutenant bars off, and took all identification out of his billfold and buried it. He swore everyone of them to secrecy, so they wouldn't reveal that he was an officer if they were captured.

The men began to talk to the German prisoner. They were going to go capture a pill box for themselves. The prisoner agreed to do it, but he was pretty sly. He led them close to a pill box, and suddenly jumped up and ran, getting back into the pill box. Bannon related this story to me. They knew that they had made a mistake. There were several Germans with burp guns who came out shooting, but somehow, Bannon told me, bullets went all around him and miraculously missed him. He was at really close range. I don't know why, but none of the GI's had the courage or reaction quick enough to shoot him. Consequently, Bannon and the other boys got away and went back up the trench and spent their time until we moved out.

Long about mid-evening we kept hearing reports that the 15th Infantry Regiment was held back in reserve, and they were pinned down, too, with the first row of pill boxes. During the day we saw Iron Mike flying over in a piper cub. He was the commander general of the division.

We got word, that there was chow. I volunteered to go get some rations. We found the chow! We weren't told that we were out of the trap, but anyway this is one instance where I wasn't being told anything. I didn't know what was going on. Old Katz called out for me to get my platoon together, and go up in this ditch and guard it. I never did answer him. I don't know what happened. Finally, there were German stragglers coming down around our pill box, and we were shooting all through the night. During this type of thing, harassment, we really didn't know what was going on. We heard later that it was Patton's breakthrough that really saved our hide. However, it was the 30th Infantry Regiment that broke through and gave us the relief that we needed.

We spent two solid days, the 18th and 19th, under very severe and difficult situations, being exposed to all types of shelling, sniping, and machine gun fire. Nobody knew what we were doing. I can't quite reconstruct this. I don't know why they would do that. In reading the history book, I understand the plans were changed by Army Headquarters. The 1st Battalion was given the section of the Siegfried Line where it was the strongest and toughest, because of the heavy casualties that the 2nd and 3rd Battalions had suffered in Utwiler.

We got up the next day, and everything had quieted down. We found out that everything was clear. Every now and then, we'd still find a German straggler soldier. We really didn't know what was going on, because we weren't kept abreast of things. In looking back to our knowledge, we hadn't had any plans for breaking the Siegfried Line, no strategy whatsoever. It was our perseverance and perhaps our purpose to disorganize the Germans, and they used other troops to break through. Anyway, they said that we were moving out about mid-day. It might have been close to mid—afternoon. We got ready to move out. The Army already had the bulldozers and engineers up there, and they already had set some dynamite charges and explosives. As we left, they were blowing those pill boxes up.

We went on to the town of Zweibbruken, which I understand was about the size of Memphis. It had about 300,000 people back in 1945. It was a good sized city. We entered the town, and we were in such a state of shock that it took us days to get our sanity back. I don't think I ever got over that. All of us were jumpy and nervous. We were tense, and you could set us off with the wrong word. There was a young woman who came out of a house. We started talking to her. She ran, and one of the GI's shot her in the leg. I don't know who did this, but I wasn't sympathetic. We wanted to kill all of them.

An old man pushing a cart came by. We had a former supply sergeant, named Roper. He was the most easygoing guy, that I've ever run across. He never got angry or upset. Roper told the old man to put his hands up. He wouldn't do it! He was trying to talk to us, but we didn't know what he was saying. Roper got a hold of him and shook, slapped and beat him up pretty good. I think this will explain to you how keyed up we were. I don't know what we did with the old man. I think we took him prisoner and congregated all the civilians in one place. We didn't trust anyone since the severe shellacking that we had taken in the last three days. Really, for five days, we'd been in some very tough fighting.

We got in a house, and we began to relax. As always, rumors began. You'd always hear rumors. They were always bad ones. Replacements came, and I had to go out and receive them. I gave them a little talking to and assigned them to their squad. They told me later, after the war, that I was the toughest looking sergeant that they had ever seen, and I really knew how to talk tough.

About March 2nd we left Zweibbruken. Our assembly area was in the vicinity of Contwig and at 2100 hours, we attacked the northeast. I don't remember the details. We were moving so fast on this attack that we cleared several towns: Batwiler, Smitenhousen, Rochenburg, Hersburg, Shieburg and Hoenog. We captured more than 100 prisoners in the process. We didn't have too much opposition. I think our 3rd Battalion probably did. They got Dallechen Weiler.

We were really moving fast, and we were hearing all kinds of reports. We got the Stars and Stripes. Somehow, they'd gotten the paper to us. We were going from town to town, blazing away, and there wasn't really any real serious opposition. Any time you have machine guns, mortar and artillery shooting at you, it's tough, but we had the Germans on the run. Hitler was furious and complaining about the Americans joyriding over the fatherland in tanks. A lot of the times we'd get on the tanks and hang on, and they'd barrel down the road, and we would run into a fight. We'd get down and take care of it, knock it out, and proceed on. This went on, and on, and on. A lot of folks back in the States thought the war was over. But it wasn't! There were still people getting killed.

We really didn't have much opposition as the Rhine River had not been crossed. This was on the 22nd. We fought a couple of days, and on the night of March 23, 1945, they moved us up to cross the Rhine River, but we didn't know it. We didn't know what we were to do until the night of the 24th. We actually crossed the Rhine River on the 26th. I recall that night, that Lieutenant Sauer was back, along with Sergeant Greene, from the rest camp. Sauer was in a joyful mood. He had some Scotch. Do you know that the officers got liquor rations? He gave Greene and I a drink. I didn't like it! I never did like Scotch. It had some kind of taste that didn't appeal to me.

That night I got official recognition that I was a staff sergeant. Then, we were briefed about crossing the Rhine River by night, and we were assigned 12 men to a boat. We were to go down at the jump-off time. There would be an engineer with each boat to crank the motor and carry us across. As we started moving out toward the river, I don't know how far it was, the German shelling began. The closer we got to the bank, the more intense it became.

The engineers had, after dark, been moving this equipment up for us to cross on. No doubt that notified the Germans of what was going to happen, but I'm telling you when we got down there, the German artillery was terrific. I've never to seen anything like it! You could hear men screaming, as they were being hit; many were killed. I don't know how we survived, because it was severely intense artillery fire. I don't know which one I could say was the worst, because I had been under heavy artillery fire in the Colmar Pocket, on the Meurthe River, and numerous other places, but they really meant business here, just like they did at the Siegfried Line. It was indescribable! There was so much shelling going on. The acrid powder scent would hit your nostrils, as explosions went on all around you. Men were crying out in pain, being hit. It was tough! I thought that we'd never survive. After we picked up our boat, all of us got under it. It was a pretty good sized boat. We carried it on our shoulders and placed it in the water. The engineer got in, and we shoved off into the water.

We started directly across, and a machine gun opened fire on us. Many more boats were getting into the water. This engineer was a little bit gun shy. He wouldn't go directly into that machine gun. He veered down to the left. We got to the bank. Fortunately, we didn't get hit. That was in his favor, certainly, but we all got out of the boat. We climbed the bank and it was a steep slope. It had some sort of slag or rocks. This was the city of Sandhofen, which we were landing by. He carried us so far to the left, that we ran into a company of the 3rd Battalion. I was a sergeant and Sergeant Bunn was there. We identified ourselves to the lieutenant in charge. We told him what had happened, and that we would like to join him. He said the only way we could join them, was to be the first scouts. That was customary. We told him, "No, thank you." Rather than do that, we'd find our own outfit, or take care of ourselves. Turning our backs on him, we walked off.

We saw the town of Sandhofen and heard firing going on. We knew there was bound to be some of our buddies there, because the 3rd Battalion was on our left, and we were the two assault battalions of the 7th Regiment. The 7th Regiment's right flank was exposed; that will tell you what a bad position we were really in. The 45th Division must have been on our left. The 3rd and 45th Divisions spearheaded the river crossing. The 7th Infantry spearheaded for the third. I don't know what other regiments did, but the 1st and 3rd Battalions spearheaded for the 7th Regiment. Charlie Company was the original assault troops to cross. We headed down back to our right and walked across an open field. It was a little after daybreak.

We could smell the fumes of artillery shells and a real battle was going on with all kinds of weapons being used by both sides.

As we came up to some houses, our men saw us, and they were real happy to see us. We went on in and joined them. Somehow, Lieutenant Sauer and Lieutenant Katz didn't get across the river in that initial assault. They came over later on, the next day. But both of them got Silver Stars and high decorations, high awards for the action they didn't participate in. Greene got the Silver Star, because he allegedly led the group, and organized them. I wasn't with our platoon, when he did this. I was talking to Greene finding out what our situation was, and it was only part of the company, being the 1st and 4th Platoons, and members of the 3rd Platoon. We were all mixed up. We were not organized. I asked Greene what was going on, and he said, "Well, right here across the street is enemy territory." We had the house on the corner, and some of our other buddies, from the other platoons, had the one across the street on the same side. That was our toehold. Greene said, "Craft, I've got an outpost. There's a long trench out there, and I'd appreciate it if you'd check on them and see if they are functioning and not asleep." I ran down to the ditch to find the guys on the outpost. A dead German was lying flat on his face in the ditch.

He was pretty tall, but even as short as I was, the first time I didn't have the courage to step on him; I jumped over him. That was a pretty good jump for me. I got on down there and talked to the guys. They were doing their job, and they told me what had happened to this Kraut. He was an officer. He jumped out of the ditch with a bunch of his men, when they originally entered the place and started shooting. The first guy to react was the guy with a bazooka. He shot the German officer in the belly with a bazooka. It did not explode! It penetrated his stomach and killed him. He fell face first with that fin sticking out. His back was arched, because of the bazooka shell, with the fin and all. The bazooka shell was approximately a foot long. When I went back, I tried to jump over the corpse again, but I misjudged my jump, stepping on his back. Air apparently came out of his mouth, making an eerie noise. This was repeated numerous times, as the outpost was checked frequently. I went back and reported to Greene that everything was all right out there, and the boys were on the ball.

There was a lot of shooting already going on. The Germans were shelling us, and in a little while Private Ance, who spoke fluent German being of German descent, brought up three women he had found in the cellar. They had been talking to some German soldiers through the wall, which was very thin, and were digging in the dirt to let them come in and catch us by surprise. When he told me that, I became furious. The oldest woman seemed to be the leader, and I slapped her very thoroughly, gave her a back-handed slap, rocking her head back and forth. I told Ance, "There's a bathroom on the third floor. Go up and lock them up, because we cannot trust them and do not have any one available to constantly guard them."

There were always some guys that do things you can never explain. Later in the day, they went across the street to loot some houses. There was some kind of playground near, and they went in the house. They were looting on the second floor. The Germans came in on the first floor, and they couldn't come downstairs. They were about to be captured, and they hollered out the window; began crying for us to come and get them out. We wouldn't do it, but one of their buddies decided to go to their rescue, and he did. He went over across the street and started shooting in the ground floor and the Germans ran. Before he went to the rescue, we knew that they were telling the truth, because there was a German who came around the side of that house and ran all the way around the house. All of us opened up on him, but it's hard to hit a man running in a sideways motion from where you're shooting. He wasn't running straight. He was an impossible target. If he'd been running away from me, I could have hit him, but I missed, as did the machine guns. Anyway, those looters were freed.

We captured some German prisoners and some that were trying to surrender. They reached the middle of the street, and their own soldiers shot one down. One of their medics went out to doctor him, and he, too, was shot. Enemy shelling became very severe, and we didn't have enough room in our place for prisoners. They had space at the other house for our six prisoners. I told a new recruit, "Take them across the street to the other house. It'll give us a little more freedom over here." I cleared it with Sergeant Bunn. The young man was marching them out single file. The house across the street from us had an embankment. They had to climb up the bank. They were a little slow, and the Krauts began to throw artillery in. This young recruit prodded the prisoner ahead of him in the rear — he did it two or three times — and the German reached back and grabbed hold of the gun and began to shake it. I don't think he was trying to pull it out of the man's hand, but the young raw recruit thought he was, and he shot him. The German let out a blood curdling death yell, a scream. It sounded pitiful. Then the other prisoners began moving faster. The young man came back and got sick. We told him him not to think anything about it. He didn't do anything wrong. Nevertheless, he felt badly about it for several days.

About nightfall the town was burning, and the other elements of the battalion had gotten together. They came and got us and we all assembled. We had to walk through the town. Sandhofen was the most unbelievable town. It was burning! We went from house to house, building to building, through an underground trench, from cellar to cellar, almost all the way through the town. You could see German helmets, swastikas, and all kind of Nazi paraphernalia as we walked through the basements. I don't know what that meant, other than it was probably a good Nazi town for Hitler. Sandhofen was finally cleared of the enemy, and we left it burning.

After leaving the town, we went to a cigar factory and smoked cigars. There was a lull, and we were left behind the other two battalions in our regiments to maintain control until the rear echelon came and took over.

CHAPTER 19
FIGHTING IN GERMANY

The fighting in Germany was a lot different from what we had been through, because the Krauts were on the run. We were traveling so fast day and night, it was hard to actually remember the names of the towns. From March 29 until the end of the war, we only had three people that I knew that were killed. After the Rhine River crossing, the serious fighting was really over. However, there were still people being killed and wounded. I do not know the exact losses.

I do remember being in the cigar factory overnight. We moved out by truck somewhere, went to the main river, and the 2nd and 3rd Battalions of the 7th Regiment were in the attack. The 2nd Battalion had already crossed that river two or three times. We pulled up into another town.

From there, we really moved. We walked, rode on tanks, trucks, ducks, and we were piled into jeeps; just any mode of transportation that was available to be used.

We crossed the main river some time during the night. We walked all night and through the next day. Apparently, we were spread pretty thin, because we were fighting on company strength. We cleared another little town, which didn't have over a dozen houses in it. Everything was quiet. We started out across a field to a highway. We had just gotten out of the little town down to a hollow, or valley. We got to the bottom of the hill in the valley, and there was an incline going up towards the woods. But we were going the other way, towards the highway to walk down it. All of a sudden, a sniper shot rang out, and Sergeant Ronnie was hit in the neck. He screamed and fell down dead. We knew it was a sniper, and everyone hit the ditch for cover. The whole company got in the ditch and started firing. Lieutenant Katz, the company commander, called on the radio, and I answered it. He wanted to speak to Sergeant Greene. Greene answered the radio. He told Greene to take the 1st Platoon and go up and get the sniper. Greene told him, "You are crazy as hell. I'm not taking my platoon up there." I don't know why old Katz didn't bring action against Greene, but he didn't. He called in the artillery and bombarded the place.

Then Katz ordered the tank to fire a number of rounds and strafe the area with machine guns. They did; then the whole company charged. We went to the place where the sniper was and found his gun. It was a sniper rifle. We tested it out. It had the telescopic lens, and you could put the mark on a man, squeeze the trigger, and you couldn't help but hit the target. The rifle had blood on it. I picked the rifle up and sighted targets with it. I would liked to have brought that rifle home with me, but I knew I couldn't. I had already lost those good field artillery glasses. Anything extra to carry was excess baggage.

We cleared that whole wooded area, looking for the sniper, and then we went on into the next town. By that time, it was getting close to dark. We hauled in the mayor with quite a few of the townspeople, questioning them about the sniper. We knew that he was hiding in the town. After searching many of the houses, we never found him. I hope he died a horrible death. To this day I would liked to have gotten my hands on him, because there is nothing that I hated worse than a sniper. I think everybody felt that way, because snipers were hidden and concealed. Sniper rifles wouldn't miss, and it was a frightening experience. I don't know where we went, because we were going so fast that it was very difficult to remember the names of the towns.

The afternoon of April 10, we had been riding tanks all day fighting the enemy. I was sitting on the rear of a tank. We went over a bridge. The bridge fell in, and the tank following us overturned, pinning three men underneath. The other men on the tank lifted it up, and Private First Class Bruce pulled the bodies from beneath it, but poor Sergeant Powers was dead. He was lying stretched out on the ground. One of his own platoon members reached down for his billfold to loot it, but one of Powers' best friends, Private First Class Bruce, threw his gun on the looter, and said, "You dirty son-of-a-bitch. You are the lowest scum that ever walked the face of this earth. If you even attempt to loot him, I'll kill you." The guy quit. We continued on in the attack against the enemy, and about 5:00 p.m. we halted in an open field. Orders were received to dig in for defense purposes. We'd been getting messages through the Stars and Stripes that Hitler was really raising cain, because the American tanks were joyriding over the "fatherland."

The Company CP sent a runner down for me, and I went back to the CP. Lieutenant Katz and the company clerk, Manfield, asked me if I'd like to go back to Nice, France, on a 10 day furlough. They said Powers, the man who was killed that afternoon, was scheduled to go. We were on a rotation basis, and I was next in line to go. I said, "Sure!" although I didn't know what I was getting into. They said it would be all right, but to answer to the name of Powers. At the time, I didn't know his first name. I only knew his name was Powers, and I was not given any other information about him.

While at the CP, I saw this Spanish boy from my platoon. He was our runner and I asked him, "What are you doing here?" He replied, "I came up to tell how Draughn got killed." Well, that happened when we first entered Germany. I knew the circumstances about it, and I was wondering why they were taking a statement from him, rather than from me. I knew that this young man, along with a lot of other youngsters, really hated Sergeant Bulin.

I had heard them say that Bulin shot Draughn, but I knew this man didn't know any more about it than I did. I knew the experiences I had had with him, because he and Galahad were both going out too far in front of their squad and not keeping proper contact. It happened like I had warned them that it would. He got out too far and I'm reasonably sure Bulin could have shot him, because he thought he was a German, as the enemy did open fire on us. It may have been the Germans who shot him, I don't know. Neither did this young man, but I think he was up there to make a statement that Sergeant Bulin did it. It made me angry. I said, "I was there when it happened."

Lieutenant Katz and the 1st sergeant replied, "Fine, you're just the man we want." I related to them what had happened, that Draughn was a scout, and it was at night, under thick underbrush. He had gotten out in front of his squad and platoon, and the Germans opened up with their machine guns. There was a fire fight and in the final analysis, Draughn was dead. I assumed the Germans killed him. If looks of hatred could have killed me, this young Hispanic would have killed me, because they told him, "We don't need any further statement from you. Sergeant Craft has already given us the information needed." I went back, told my men and the platoon sergeant what had happened, and that I was going to the rest camp on the Riviera. I took my equipment and turned it in to the supply department. They put another man, named Russo, from the 3rd Platoon in a jeep with me, and he carried us to the Regimental Headquarters. From there, we got on a truck and we went back to the Division Headquarters. In order to help financially, the payroll people were paying all the men going on furlough. They were trying to pay Powers, and they'd call the roll every time we'd stop, and I'd answer 'here', as his name was called.

Back at the Division Headquarters, they were calling, "Powers, Powers," because they knew he needed some money, but I kept silent, because I didn't want to answer any questions. After the roll call was completed, they kept calling Powers' name. I still did not answer, because to receive the money I had to sign his name, and I knew this would present a legal problem. We were first transported by truck, and then put on a train.

On the truck we went through Colmar and the Black Forest that overlooked Strasbourg. I only had a glimpse of Colmar from the covered truck looking out the back. We finally got to a railroad depot, got on a troop train, and then we headed down to southern France. We stopped once at a railroad yard. I don't know where it was. They had two captured German railroad guns parked in the railway yard. That was very interesting to me, since we thought we had experienced some fire thrown from one of them in the Siegfried Line. We went up and inspected the guns, and poked our heads in them. At that time, I could get my body up into the barrel, where the shell is loaded. I was afraid to attempt to go all the way through, because I did not want to get hung up in the barrel. The gun barrel was longer than a standard boxcar.

We returned to the troop train. Music was coming from the loud speaker. It was interrupted, and they announced that President Roosevelt had died. The train stopped shortly thereafter, and we all got out. This news jarred us. In our eyes, he hung the moon. We thought his death might delay the end of the war. Some of the guys cried. However, we got back on the troop train, and went on to Nice, France. Before we got there, they let the officers off at Cannes. This was the officer's camp. We enlisted men had to go on to Nice. You see, again, the discrimination! The officers had better quarters and facilities, etc., but I think, perhaps, it was for the best, because we had a better time, not having to fool with them.

We stayed in one of the finer hotels, overlooking the Mediterranean Sea. Russo went to the supply room and got clean clothes, a razor and some shaving cream. He loaned me his razor. I didn't have much to shave, but I was filthy. My clothes were dirty and I was afraid to get out, knowing the MP's would pick me up for being a deserter. I didn't know what to do, and I talked it over with Russo. We decided that it was best for me to seek help. There was a colonel, who was in charge of the hotel. The bulletin board stated that if you had any problems, to come see him. I talked it over with Russo — all of the pros and cons. I really didn't know what to do. Finally, I got up enough nerve and walked in to see the colonel. He graciously allowed me an audience. I told him the truth. I informed him that I had been in combat for a long, long time, since November 1, 1944, and my company commander and clerk explained to me that we had a rotating furlough, which was based on the length of time in combat. Because of Army red tape, when someone got killed that was on the furlough roster, they could not substitute someone in his place; that I was next in line after Powers' furlough ended. I told the colonel that they neglected to give me all the information on him.

I did not have any clean clothes, or any money, because I knew it would be illegal to collect money belonging to a dead soldier. I knew I was conspicuous, and the MPs would probably pick me up. He understood my plight, saying, "Sergeant, you deserve a rest. I'm not blaming you in the least. But, technically, you're AWOL." I replied, "I am! Well, if I'm AWOL, the company clerk and my company commander know where I am. In my mind, I'm not, because I wouldn't have left unless I had been approved." He replied, "Well, you go ahead and enjoy yourself. I'm going to give you a pass to go down and get yourself some clothes. You have an enjoyable stay here." I didn't know the peckerwood was going to report it to the Army Headquarters. I went on and enjoyed myself. I couldn't draw any pay, and I didn't have any money on me. I was flat broke! We hadn't been paid since we'd gone on the lines, but Russo was kind enough to lend me 50 dollars. I'd just met him on this trip, and that's how much trust he had in me. I said, "Well, Russo, tell me where you live, in case something happens to you. I can mail it to your family." He replied, "No, we came down together as buddies, and we're going to have a good time on this money."

We had a lovely time, taking rides in a horse-drawn carriage and a two-wheel cart attached to a bicycle called "taxis." I have a photograph, taken in Nice, of me near the bicycle taxi. Somehow, in the period of combat, in the midst of all those hardships, I had gained weight. I weighed 160 pounds, and found it hard to believe. I know 50 dollars, even at that time, wasn't much money on the Riviera, but everything we wanted to do, we did, and we had 10 dollars each left over. We ate good, hot food and could have gone swimming in the Mediterranean Sea, if we had wanted to, but we didn't.

We saw a lot of beautiful women on the Riviera. That was my first experience of seeing women with hair all different colors. The following was really outstanding: I saw a girl that had really long hair, in fact, all of them wore their hair that way, down below their shoulders; some of them down to their waist; some below their hips. This particular one had purple hair. No doubt, it was dyed. Russo spoke fluent French. He was born and reared on the Canadian border. He told me that he couldn't speak English until he went to school. His father and mother both spoke French.

In our contact with the French, he would usually initiate the conversation by speaking in French. Somehow I didn't seem too get along to well with those people. I'm sure the language barrier was one reason. One day we were fooling around and ran across a pretty girl, a brunette. I don't remember her name. Russo approached her and spoke in French, saying "Parlez vous Francai?" which means, "Do you speak French?" She laughed and replied in English, "Yes, I speak French and I understand English. Perhaps we'd better stay with English." It embarrassed Russo. We invited her out for a drink which was served in a bar under a long tent, which wasn't uncommon over there. Drinks, food, and anything you wanted was in open shelter. The only intoxicant Russo and I could drink, because of finances, was Vermouth, which we drank until it came out of our ears. It is some kind of sweet wine and didn't have much kick to it. I really got sick from it and have not drunk any since. We had a delightful chat with the young lady and went on about our way.

During this time we could see movies, and we'd go to night clubs. I remember one night we went to a club which had a good band and that sort of thing. All the GIs were there relaxing from the front lines. There was a Frenchman, shorter than I, who was drunk. He was going around hugging all the GIs and kissing them, as is the French custom, really making a nuisance of himself. I immediately formed a dislike to him, and I thought to myself, "If that damn Frenchman comes up and tries to hug and kiss me, I'm gonna knock the hell out of him." I believe the Frenchman sensed that, because he came up and looked me right in the eye, and even though he was drunk, he didn't touch me. I might have caused a commotion there that night if he had, because my love of drunks wasn't too high. I wasn't impressed with them. Fortunately, he didn't! He went on about his way. We had a good time and relaxed.

When the 10 days were over, we got on a troop train heading back to the dreadful front lines where pain, fear and death would prevail once again. We arrived in Nancy, and we were told that it was going to be hard to get transportation out. They were trying to get supplies to the advancing elements. In Nancy, a map was posted on the wall, with different towns marked on it. Every day, we would go by to look at it, because the map was constantly changing. It showed you where your division was. The 3rd Division was fighting in Nuremberg. I understand that they had quite a battle. In fact, one of our men was killed there.

Incidentally, on this subject: while I wasn't there something happened to one of our good cooks, who was an arrogant and overbearing person. I guess the cooks were staying pretty close to us then, or perhaps that was after Nuremberg was taken. This is the story that was related to me: He went out one night and raped a German woman. That goes to show you that the guy was a fool. You didn't have to rape any of the European women, as they were sex hungry, and they did not need much encouragement to sleep with the GIs. He supposedly raped her, and she reported it to the company commander. He had our company in formation with their helmets off, and let her go down the line, looking at each individual. She picked out the cook. They were going to court-martial him.

That night, the crazy fool went out on the town, and he was found dead on the street. Apparently, the Germans had either shot or knifed him. I don't remember which, but the boy died, and it was a shame. I don't know of that ever happening in our outfit but that one time. It was incredible! I couldn't believe it, because like I said, it was hard for me to believe that you had to rape these women. They did not think sleeping with any man was wrong.

While waiting in Nancy, we had a good room with a warm bed. We had hot chow, and the only thing that we were doing was sweating out the end of the war. Our time came to leave, and we were loaded into trucks and headed out for Germany. We went back through Army Headquarters and Division Headquarters. When I got to the Regiment, I was on the truck. They called out over a loud speaker for Sergeant Craft to report to Major somebody. I went in to see him, and I introduced myself. He said, "Have a seat. What's this I hear about you?" I said, "I don't quite understand, Major." He replied, "Well, I have a report here from the Army Headquarters, that you went on a furlough in someone else's place." I said, "Oh, yes sir, I did." He questioned me as to who gave me the authority, and I told him. Then he replied, "Well, don't worry about it. Go on back to your outfit. I'll check it out." I don't know whether he did, or what happened, but the company clerk must have lost his job, because he was put in our platoon, and he never said anything about it. His name was Manfield. He was a good fellow, and he was very conscientious. He was doing a good job, but he made his mistake in not giving me complete information on who I was impersonating. I regretted his demotion, but I don't know of any other way that the matter could have been handled. Even today, I think they were remiss in not giving me the complete information so that I could properly impersonate Powers.

The Regiment was in Augsburg, Germany, and we went and joined our company. They had just taken the town. We spent the night there, and the next day we headed for our next objective: Munchen (Munich). We saw the road signs showing it was 70 kilometers. That is about 43 miles. I was told that in taking Augsburg, the Division pulled up a short distance from town, and they tried to negotiate a surrender with the Krauts, without tearing it down. Even though the civilians were involved, they could not persuade the German officers in command to do so. Then the civilians took matters in their own hands, and they hung 12 officers. The city was surrendered without too much gunfire. I understand that Albert Speer, Hitler's second in command, visited the Army officers on the day before it was captured. His mission, allegedly, was to preserve the city. We left Augsburg on foot, and we were informed that this was going to be a mad rush to capture Munich. We set out walking and were told that they didn't have enough vehicles to transport everybody.

They'd haul a battalion or two with what vehicles were available, and take them up several miles. They'd unload them and then come back and get us. The battalion rotated in that manner. I recall this march to Munich was pretty tough; but we were making good time. We were in a hurry and walking through little towns as if there was no enemy. There was a little shooting every now and then. I recall, too, that for some reason, at one place we decided to take a break. As usual, there would be a platoon of men to a house, in order to keep everybody intact. We went into a home, and commandeered it. We put a woman and her family in one of the bedrooms, and went into the kitchen. Old Bernie was off looting again. He and some of his buddies found a warehouse and brought back a case of eggs. We began to search around the house and found hams, bacon, black bread and marmalade. We found some frying pans in the pantry. Everyone was cooking for himself. We sliced the ham and bacon, and fried it. It was good ham, done in a big skillet. Everyone was using every available pan to fry their food. I cooked my eggs sunny side up. I cracked four, put them in the pan, got some ham and toast, made with dark bread, and marmalade. We had two or three pieces of toast to each serving. I cooked and ate 13 fried eggs with a big slice of ham and two or three pieces of toasted bread with what they called butter (it was nothing but fat), along with the marmalade. I've never been so hungry or enjoyed a meal so much in all my life, because we'd been walking all day long. This occurred after mid-day.

This is the place where we were waiting on trucks. Before we left, this little incident might be of interest to whomever reads this:

We were making such a mess and commotion in the lady's kitchen, that she became quite upset. She came into the kitchen and said, "Please, please, let me do the cooking for you. You're making too big of a mess." Being the sergeant, I explained that we were not supposed to fraternize with her, or any Germans. I was sorry for the mess, but she would have to bear with it, and just go back to the bedroom.

Before I forget this: We were in a town, shortly after we entered Germany. As we approached a good sized city on foot, the German civilians saw us, and they were terrified. They thought that we were Russians. When they found out that we were Americans, they were really overjoyed. It was a case similar to the first one I just related to you. We went into a house which was three stories high. This woman was a rich person, probably a Nazi. She had four bedrooms on the third floor, and several bedrooms on the second floor. It was modern and up-to-date, and it was spic and span. This incident happened before I went on my furlough to Nice. We talked with her, and she told us, "The Germans and the Americans really aren't enemies. The Russians are the real enemy. You all are going to push the German soldiers against the Russians, and then the Germans are going to turn around, and all of us are going to fight the Russians." We laughed, thinking it was hilarious. We thought the Russians were our allies. At that time we didn't know anything about Communism or Joseph Stalin's methods.

We ate, then went upstairs to the bedroom. Boy, I'm telling you, the bedroom I was in had twin beds, and you can imagine if you look at some of the pictures in the history book how dirty we were. She had the nice beds made up to perfection with a fancy comforter on them. These comforters had feathers in them to keep warm. I guess they did conserve fuel. Anyway, the guy with me flopped down, boots and all, on the bed. Naturally, that wasn't rude to us, because we wouldn't take off our clothes. We were subject to be called to move out on a moment's notice. I was lying back, propped up, had my pillow doubled up, lying there relaxing, shooting the bull with this guy on the bed next to me, and she came and peeked through the door. When she looked in, I saw the look of horror on her face. Here were these GIs, dirty, and on her fine bed and linens. I understood the woman's feelings. She didn't say a word, but I could tell what the look meant. I immediately thought, "Could I do this to my mother?" She left, not saying anything about it. I don't recall ever seeing her again, but I do know that when we left all those Germans gathered around telling us good-bye, and that they were glad that we were not the swartz or the dark colored Americans. They were talking about the American Negroes.

The trucks came back for us and drove us on into Munich. The 1st Battalion spearheaded the drive. I don't recall, really, a shot being fired, to tell you the truth. I remember the elaborate air defenses that they had surrounding the town, and pictures don't lie, because that was the most awesome defense system that I have ever seen. I don't see how an airplane could get through. We stayed in Munich a day or two, and we were confined to a certain sector. Munich was a big town, and we couldn't stray too far away. We had one guy, Ance, and another, who was an Indian Chief. Ance was of German descent; the chief was an Indian, and a Casanova. He could go out and get a woman when nobody else could find one. I think all French and German women certainly did like Indians and Negroes.

If I may, at this point, go back to November 30, when we were in Strasbourg, the night before we crossed a railroad to knock out a pocket of Germans. Johnny Clayton was in the 2nd Platoon. He was my good buddy from Bethel Springs, Tennessee, and he was on patrol to cross this bridge. They did get across the bridge, but the Germans were waiting for them. They got in pretty close fighting. However, they had to retreat, because there was so much resistance. Johnny killed several Germans there, and he was awarded the Silver Star.

I left out another incident. Sometime after we crossed the Rhine River and left Sandhofen, we had orders that when we took a town or commandeered a house, or took possession of a house for temporary quarters, to put the Germans in one room and not to let them out. There was to be no fraternization at all because it was expected that the civilians would have all kinds of tricks to thwart the invasion. The infantrymen on the front lines, for a number of reasons, had the toughest job of all. Because of the walking that they had to do, the exposure to the weather, rain, snow, sleet, wind and mud, usually the infantry was the first ones to make contact with the enemy, or at least to scatter or overrun them. We had orders not to loot when we hit Germany, but it became an obsession with some. We were all guilty to a certain degree of looting. My looting was primarily confined to finding food.

Whenever we went into a house or a town, we searched to find eggs. The Germans called eggs "Ires." We were looking for something quick to cook, such as eggs, ham, bacon, bread and marmalade. That's where I learned to like marmalade, in Germany. I remember once in a small village, after taking possession of a house and putting the man, his wife and girls in a back bedroom, we searched and searched for eggs. We couldn't find any food. Back in the bedroom this German had a churn, similar to the one my mother used when I was growing up. It was full of milk, and one of the boys opened it up. He ran his hand down in the milk and found some eggs. I noticed that the man of the house had gone outside. He had a great, big horse and was hitching him up to a one-horse wagon. I went out to investigate, and this fellow Ance, who could speak fluent German, came up. I had tried to talk to the old German. I know now, that he was very angry. He pretended that he didn't understand me. I knew Ance could get to him, and I told Ance to tell him to unhitch the horse; and to get back in the house quickly. We weren't going to put up with any foolishness. After Ance repeated the instructions to the man, he unhitched the horse from the wagon, and carried him down to the barn, located in their basement. Ance went down to check on him, and the old German had already put the horse up, but he had a pistol out and had it up to his head, and he was going to shoot himself. Ance stopped him, and made him give up the pistol. I don't know whatever happened to the gun. I had so many other things on my mind other than this. He came back and brought him up to me and told me what had happened, and I told Ance to tell him he was to go to the bedroom and stay, and if he got out of there again, we were going to put him up by the side of the house and shoot not only him, but his whole family. I was tired of fooling around with him. He marched the old man at gunpoint back into the house. We didn't have any more trouble out of him.

We stayed there several more hours. Shortly after noon, the trucks came and picked us up. We continued on our journey through Germany, to fight the Krauts and clear out the rest of it. I don't know the name of this town. As we left, the old man came out, he had gotten his horse and hitched it to his wagon. He was leaving, too. I don't know where in the world he was going. I always wondered. Nevertheless, that was another anecdote that happened. It was a little aggravating to me to be in charge of the troops. I understand how the old man felt, but nevertheless, this was war and we were victors; he was the loser. He had to take and accept things, too. We had our orders and had to protect ourselves. We chose to carry instructions out for our own safety.

While we were in Munich, in the latter part of April 1945, our Platoon Sergeant Greene was having trouble with both Ance and the chief, whose name was Martin. Both of them wanted to play by their own rules. Ance had been used to coax the Germans to surrender; he may have, in anger, shot some in cold blood. It was about to break him. The chief, as we called him, was just a happy-go-lucky guy and eventually, he disappeared. I don't know where he went. I never did know what happened to Ance, either.

One afternoon, we got a bunch of leaflets to pass out for each man in our platoon. In this leaflet, it stated that the 3rd Division had been chosen to make an attack on a redoubt center. It was a secretive mission. They suspected

CHAPTER 20
CAPTURING BERCHTESGADEN

We got into trucks again, and headed toward Salzburg, Austria. At that time I was neither aware of the name of Salzburg, or Berchtesgaden, which was Hitler's hideout.

On May 1, we got the orders to move, and we were loaded onto trucks and moved out. We had been riding all night. I recalled songs being written about the Blue Danube, and I remembered learning about this river while in elementary school, back in Smith County. I was awake at the time we crossed. The river was as blue and beautiful as I had it pictured.

We crossed the bridge, got on a road, and all of a sudden, I got sleepy. I was sitting at the rear of the truck, and I laid my head on somebody's leg and dozed off. In that short time, I had a very vivid dream. This was my second dream I can recall having while in combat. In this dream, the flash of the Blue Danube crossed my mind, and I dreamed we were on our way to a port to go back to the United States. I was so happy. I was disappointed when I woke up and found myself still on a truck, heading for the Redoubt Center. We didn't know what we were going to encounter. The picture of the Redoubt Center had been painted pretty bleak — an ugly picture. But we made a mad rush. At some point, the trucks stopped and put us out. All along the way on the autobahn for miles and miles, there were German airplanes on each side of the autobahn. The autobahn was something like the expressways we have today. We were really traveling fast. I don't know how great the distance, but we got off the autobahn. We began hitting some opposition. We were traveling on tanks, trucks and ducks. My platoon was in a duck. We merely blazed right on through one little town after little town, hitting some opposition. We'd get stopped every now and then by machine gun fire, and the Germans had their roadblocks. We'd knock them out and proceed on; they might have a bridge knocked out. We'd have to wait and let a bridge be put up, or be repaired, then proceed on. I can recall seeing German soldiers out in the fields and the meadows, and we'd try to coax them to surrender and give up their arms. When they wouldn't do it, we'd cut down on them with our guns shooting from whatever vehicle we were on.

We came to a town. I don't remember its name or the day. Just outside of it was a canal that had to be crossed, and the bridge had been blown. The Germans had several machine guns set up around the bridge. We didn't bother with knocking it out. I guess, the higher-ups thought, "Well, we'll just let them rest a while." We didn't really consider it serious. Apparently, they had called back for the engineers to come up and repair the bridges. We were in the town, loafing, looting, and sleep was beyond the question. We were too excited, and as I recall, we could look out and see the bridge that had been knocked out. The engineer company came barging on through the town. The lead elements were a half track and two jeeps behind it. They barged right through the town, through us, and as they approached the knocked out bridge, those German machine guns opened up fire on them. The half track made an about turn rather than boring on into them. They could have knocked them out very easily with those .50 calibers, and they had a heavy shell that they could shoot from the half track, but they didn't want to fight. The jeeps turned around, right behind it, and came back. They stopped and said, "Well, golly, there are German machine guns out there, shooting at us. What in the world is going on? We thought you infantry boys had already cleared it out." We died laughing, because we knew that we were going to have to knock them out, but we didn't have a half track, and we didn't even have a jeep with a .50 caliber on it. We had to go out there with our small M-1s and knock it out. We stayed where we were for about an hour or two. I don't know what was happening, but we walked out there and the Germans didn't even fire a shot. They gave up! I'll admit we were a big force, and they knew it was useless to resist. We crossed the bridge. Apparently, they must have gotten it repaired quickly, but we went on the rest of the afternoon, and saw nothing much, just a little sporadic fighting.

We saw hordes of German prisoners marching on the autobahn. They were by themselves. We didn't have enough troops to take care of the prisoners, who were on the honor system to go back and face the stockade. Whether that made sense or not, I don't know, but I guess that was the best that we could do.

About evening, we came near the edge of another town, the name of which I have forgotten. It had snowed that day, and as we were going into the town, an airplane, a single engine craft, took off from the airport. It was German and probably contained the big-shot Krauts. All of us were shooting at it. We had a 2nd lieutenant named Morrow, really a nice young man out of West Point, and he couldn't understand, why I was up there on the road shooting. He said, "Come on down here in the ditch, sergeant." I took a few shots at the plane, and I saw that we couldn't get him. I thought there was a bigger attack coming and got in the ditch with him.

We got in the duck, and went into town. Again, we took over another house. Later that evening, Lieutenant Morrow came around and said he wanted me to go on a patrol with him. He'd been selected to lead it. We had about eight men with us. We were to go and see if the bridge that went into Austria was intact.

We knew the war was near its end. We went on the patrol, set out through the city, not knowing whether it had been cleared or not. We got to a river bank, and rather than cross the bridge on the highway, we had been told that there was a walk bridge farther up the river, which we found. It was secure. For some reason, the lieutenant didn't want to go across it. I wouldn't have minded, but he insisted that this was all we needed to do — just to see if it was intact. We went back and he reported to the Company Headquarters, and Captain Katz really got on to him about it. We were supposed to go across there and feel it out. We were to go down and secure the main bridge on the highway, but we did not do that, and we stayed where we were that night. The past few days were beginning to get under my skin. I knew that I'd seen so much action, that it only took one sniper's bullet to get me. I guess I kind of lost my courage and bolstered it by drinking. I carried a bottle of cognac along with me. I don't know where it came from, but we were all pretty well supplied.

The next afternoon we got on trucks and weren't told where we were going, but we were headed for Berchtesgaden. Now the story behind this city of Berchtesgaden: It was Hitler's resort down in Bavaria, a pretty good sized town. It was beautiful, and it was located at the base of a mountain. Upon this mountain, Hitler had an elaborate hideout. It had been reported to us, and other sources, that the RAF had come over a few days prior and bombed his hideout, and that it was still burning. We traveled on this mountainous road to Berchtesgaden. The 1st Battalion in the 7th Infantry was spearheading it. We were in trucks. Unbeknownst to me at that time, the regimental commander, Colonel Harrington was in our group. We left the 2nd Platoon of Charlie Company on this bridge that other friendly forces were to cross, to prevent other units from beating us in the race for Berchtesgaden. It was quite an accomplishment to capture this town.

The 101st Airborne Division and the 2nd French Army were to be given that privilege. General Mike Grafton told Colonel Harrington to put the second platoon of Charlie Company with some tanks to guard the bridges and not let the French or 101st Airborne across until we had captured Berchtesgaden. Actually, the 101st Airborne Division and the 2nd French Army came up to the bridge, and our 2nd Platoon stood them off, and they wouldn't let them cross. We went on into Berchtesgaden. I don't know that a shot was fired going into the city of Berchtesgaden. I do know, that we got off the trucks and started clearing a few of the very rich houses. One place we entered had a number of German officers, and one of them came out. The Germans had a worse caste organization than the Americans had. Really, the 2nd lieutenants, the 1st lieutenants, and the captains considered it to be beneath their dignity to surrender to an enlisted man. When the German officer came out, I told him to put his hands up. He insisted that he had to surrender to an officer. I told him to keep his hands up. It didn't make any difference what his wishes were, I had the gun and if he didn't obey me, I'd shoot him. We went over and immediately looted him. He didn't have a wristwatch, but he had a gold pocket watch. I snatched that out of his vest pocket, and, boy, he screamed like a panther, but that was the only thing I got. We herded them all together, the officers and the enlisted men into one section and turned them over to somebody else. I don't know what happened to them. I didn't care!

Shortly thereafter, we had the town pretty well cleared up. We commandeered a house and our 2nd Battalion had gone on and taken Salzburg. May 3 was the day that we captured Berchtesgaden.

In Berchtesgaden, at Herman Goering staff headquarters, General Der Fleiger (Lt. Gen.) Gustav Kastner Kirkdorf was found dead in his bedroom adjoining his office, according to a female employee who was questioned. He was a member of Adolph Hitler's staff, and he had arrived at Goering's headquarters on May 2. He committed suicide shortly after we entered the town as did one other German general. Colonel Fritz Goering of the Luftwaff, who was a nephew of the #2 Nazi, Hermann Goering, personally surrendered to Colonel Harrington and personally handed his pistol to the commanding officer. Colonel Harrington questioned him about the whereabouts of Adolph Hitler, Hermann Goering and other Nazi officials. It was hoped that some of them could be captured. The German colonel said he did not know of his uncle's whereabouts, because Hitler had had Hermann Goering arrested a few days before, for wanting to quit the war; neither did he know anything about Hitler's whereabouts.

He told Colonel Harrington, that he would like to turn over to the 7th Infantry commander the property of Hermann and Frau Goering, which was quite considerable. That which interested the cottonbaler colonel the most was some 18,000 bottles of the finest liquor and two automobiles, the field marshall's two seated roadster and the 14 passenger bullet proof sedan. There was much rejoicing and excitement over the capture of Berchtesgaden, and the troops indulged in a little celebrating. Champagne and cigars were found in abundance in Hitler's and Goering's former establishment, which was also searched for souvenirs. This was apparently done by the higher ranked officers, because we didn't see it, nor did we get any of the liquor. We had to drink some old stinking wine.

On May 5, 1945, an important ceremony was held when the American flag was raised over Der Berhoff in Berchtesgaden by the 7th Infantry Division. At first, the ceremony was delayed by French interference. The French had entered Berchtesgaden near the early evening of May 4, and were given a section of the town to occupy. They really wanted to share in this honor, but it seems like their flag wouldn't work and ours went up anyway. They tried all sorts of tricks, but still their flag was too big and it dragged the ground. The French officer then withdrew his objection, and the American flag alone was raised over the Fuhrer's former mountain retreat.

CHAPTER 21
WAR IN EUROPE IS OVER

We still didn't know the war was over, officially. However, on May 5 the following message was received at the command post from the commanding general:

"Effective immediately, there will be no more fighting unless fired upon or attacked."

I believe it was really May 5, before we finally found out that the war was over. The 7th Infantry was ordered to move its 1st and 3rd Battalions from Berchtesgaden, and to assemble the entire Regiment in Salzburg, Austria. We reluctantly turned the whole place over to the 506th Parachute Regiment of the 101st Airborne Division and to the French troops, and then we moved to Salzburg, Austria. When we assembled there, the German Army began to surrender, wholesale. For days and days, the German units intact, were coming into Salzburg to surrender to the Americans, rather than to the Russians. And, incidentally, there were a lot of people other than the 3rd Division that wanted to capture Berchtesgaden. It seemed like the Russians wanted to, but they were deprived of that by the 3rd Division, and I think if the 3rd Division hadn't taken it, probably, the French and the 101st Airborne Division would have had that glorious honor.

In the dash to Salzburg and Berchtesgaden, the 3rd Division, 3rd Army, 20th Armored Division, and the Russians, too, were headed towards this famous town. I'm glad that we got it, because at least we kept the Russians and other units from having the honor of taking Hitler's hideout. A few days later, there was still a little fighting going on. We hadn't been involved in it, but it was reported that the Charlie Company was alerted to go out and knock out a pocket of Germans, who were still fighting. They didn't know the war was over. Fortunately, that never materialized, and I was delighted because I'd had my fill of fighting.

In Salzburg, we were billeted in a big apartment house. It was owned by former Nazis. A Nazi woman still lived there with her mother, and she had a big German Shepherd dog. She was on the same floor that I was, and she'd come out and take the dog for a walk, and that was all we saw of her. She was a black headed woman, not overly beautiful, but a plain woman. Salzburg was a delightful place, and it had a lot of beautiful women. It had been bombed, and there was some fighting in the city. Some of the town was destroyed, but for the most part, it was a pleasant stay. The only thing wrong was the lack of food. The quartermaster was engaged in the black market, and they had the excuse that the supply lines were long and drawn out. Consequently, we ate vegetable stew out of C-rations for breakfast, for weeks and months. As a supplement, we raided the Austrian gardens for vegetables.

One delightful thing that happened in Salzburg: — We only had to pull speed marches to keep in shape, and we'd go in the morning for an hour or two and that would be all. We'd have the rest of the day off. One time, the 1st Platoon of Charlie Company was allowed to go up into a mountain resort, owned by von Ribbentrop, the champagne salesman. It was a beautiful lodge on a lake, well equipped. There was one row boat with oars. I spent most of my time out on this lake, and it was miles long. Without life jackets, several buddies and myself, got out in it. Almost to the end of the lake, lying along the banks, were beautiful women, sunning. I guess they were Nazis, but none of them would admit it.

One afternoon, when we got back, some of the boys wanted to give me a drink of champagne. I said, "Sure, where did you get it?" and they said, "A half track came up here with a couple of trucks and a bunch of men started digging. They dug up a catch of von Ribbentrop's champagne. They loaded it on trucks and took it back to Salzburg, leaving us one case." I said, "I sure wish that I'd have been here, we'd have gotten more than a case." but, they had already gone. We consumed the case, which didn't go very far, but we had a delightful time there.

We stayed in Salzburg from May until sometime in August. It was cool there in the snow-capped mountains. We could see snow on the mountain peaks. It would melt a little each day. The first time that I ever heard it thunder or saw it lightening during my stay in Europe, a heavy rain came, and the next morning the mountains were covered with snow again.

Charlie Company was to be the honor guard for the Division Headquarters. To pull this duty, we did extensive close order drills. But the day of the parade, I came down with a high fever, and I told them that I was going to have to pass on this one, because I didn't feel well. I lay down, and when they got back, I was burning up with fever. Greene came by and felt of my face, and he saw how hot I was. He ordered an ambulance, which came and took me on a stretcher to a hospital in a huge tent. It had a lot of men in it. I was given medication. My fever went down and the next day I was feeling better, but they kept me there for a week confined to bed.

When GIs get together we relate stories about some of our experiences. They were from different companies and battalions. This was an unusual situation. Most of the infantrymen, who had any experience with the tankers did not respect them. We thought that they were yellow, because we had to go in front of them in battle to protect them. We were talking about this, and there happened to be one lone tanker soldier in the tent. He raised up, and he told us that he was from the 756th Tank Battalion; that we didn't know what we were talking about. I'm telling you, the whole group of us outnumbered him, and there were some artillery boys there, too. They joined in with us, because the artillery boys respected the infantrymen and they knew what we had to go through. We really shut this tanker up. He didn't say another word. He knew that he was outnumbered.

Later on, I had to go to the hospital again for some minor surgery — to have a wart taken off. They had to put me in the hospital to do that. I don't know why. While I was there, we were hearing all kinds of rumors and the 3rd Division got orders to go back to Germany. They were transferred while I was in the hospital. While I was in the hospital I was in Patton's area, and Patton was a chicken, because he was demanding that you wear your ties, cap, and all that kind of stuff. I didn't much go for that, but I didn't want to cross the general, so I tried to comply when I went out. While I was in the hospital, wherever it was, one day we were eating a meal. We were required to put all our medals on, and we, the 3rd Division, had received the French Fourragere and the Presidential Unit Citation for the Division and my Battalion, which occurred at Bourg-Bruche. Some of the boys were curious about these medals, and they began asking me about them. I was giving them honest answers as I knew it. There was a boy from the 82nd Parachute Division sitting at the table nearby me. I made the remark that the 3rd Division was the largest unit that ever received the Croix de Guerre with Palm and the Presidential Unit Citation. I was only quoting what I had been told. He challenged me and he was a little cocky. Rather than make an issue of it, I tried to change the subject. The guys around me took it up. They really put the paratrooper down. They shut him up and said, "The man is telling you what he's been told, and it must be true." He was claiming that the 82nd Parachute Division had gotten that, too, and they didn't believe him. They believed me.

I found out that our division was transferred. I began to inquire. I was afraid that if they got too far away from me, they might put me in another unit, and then send me to Japan, because it was rumored that the 3rd Battalion was going to stay in Germany as occupational forces. I prevailed on the doctor to let me out, so I could join my outfit, and he did.

I went back to Salzburg, and they were all gone, except parts of the Division Headquarters. I went to where we were billeted and it was empty. The jeep driver that I rode with, carried me on around to the Division Headquarters, and I talked to the people there. There was a fellow from West Memphis, Arkansas, who said that they were the last personnel left there, and they were leaving in an hour or two on a troop train; I would be welcome to ride with them back to Heidelberg, Germany. I appreciated that and I waited around. We were put in boxcars. The sergeant from West

Memphis, another fellow, and I were in a boxcar to ourselves. It took three or four days, and we had 10 and one rations to eat. We were quite comfortable, and we had a good time. We got back to Heidelberg, and I was dispatched by jeep to the Regiment, who sent me by jeep to C Company, billeted in a little cow town.

We were hurting for food, because the black market prevailed. The quartermaster was selling it on the black market to the civilians. The Company Commander, Captain Atney, called us all together and said he'd like to pass the word on to the men to ask them to donate five or 10 dollars each to a fund, and we'd go out and buy our own meat. We did, and that's the only way we had meat.

While in this little town, we didn't do anything but pull guard out on the line with the Russians, who were always giving us some kind of problems. The refugees were streaming across our lines, and we were trying to keep them from coming through. In one instance, a young man shot a woman, killing her. To keep him from being prosecuted by the civil government, our company commander court-martialed him and gave him a pardon. That was a ruse to keep him from being prosecuted by the Germans.

We pulled guard and stayed there until sometime in September. I was still a staff sergeant, and the only duty I had to pull was once a week, to post the guards at posts on the border. Our duty was to collect the ammunition and redistribute it to the new guards that we posted. One night this young boy wasn't familiar with the situation, and he, apparently, kept his ammunition, because I made records. Each time I accounted for those records and reported it to the Company Headquarters. That afternoon, this boy got off guard. He was just a young kid, and he went out in the back, where we were billeted, and he started shooting in the company area. Nobody was supposed to have any ammunition. Old Captain Atney called me in and asked me about it. I told him that I had kept a record of it, and I asked him for the ammunition, and had made my report to the Headquarters; I had my scratch sheet back, where I was billeted. He said, that I had better go find it. I went back there. Someone had emptied the waste paper can and destroyed it. I went back and told the captain that I didn't have the scratch sheet, as it had been thrown in a waste paper can, and someone had emptied the can, and my notes were destroyed. His reply was that the young man told a different story, and the captain said he was going to make an example out of me, to impress the whole company. He was going to bust me, and that I'd be reinstated. He wanted to see me as a tech sergeant, as I deserved it for my excellent combat record. I told him that rank didn't appeal to me, that I felt that my job was done. Now that the war was over, all I wanted to do was to go home.

A week or so later I had 48 points, and people from 45 points on up to the

60s were being transferred out of the 3rd Division into the 78th Division, and they were going to Berlin. I wanted to go to Berlin. My name wasn't on the roster. I raised cain with the company clerk. He said, "Well, you know why your name's not on here." I said, "Well, maybe I do and maybe I don't. I don't care, but I want to get out of this chicken outfit. I don't want any part of it any more. I want my name on that list." I guess he told Captain Atney what I had said. They put my name on the list, and I went to the 78th Division.

We went to another cow town and then into Berlin. I was always glad I did, because it was the best experience that I ever had in the service. I didn't have those sergeant stripes for them to put me in any kind of position of responsibility. I could goof off and do what I wanted to do. And that, I did! I really enjoyed my stay in Berlin. I sure gave them a hard way to go. We had to pull guard every now and then. One night, I was posted on duty to keep order at a dance hall. I was keeping order, which wasn't much of a job, unless somebody got in a fight. I wouldn't say anything to them. I was even drinking with some of my buddies, and the OD officer came around. He didn't stop, but he saw me through a window drinking. The next day an order was put out that there would be no more drinking by the guards at the dance hall. I pulled guard at several places every now and then. I remember one time that Cecil London and I were pulling guard, and we carried a bottle, and we were both half tight. The next morning, we got in about 7:00 a.m., and the boys were busy shaving, and getting their bunks made. They said, "Craft, you'd better hurry up, and get your bunk made." I asked, "What for?" They replied, "We're going to have an inspection by the battalion commander." I said, "Well, that's tough. I've been on guard." The battalion commander came around with the company commander and the platoon sergeant. I know that I embarrassed them, and I did it deliberately. They came in and yelled "Tennshut" and my bed wasn't made. I was in my underwear. The battalion commander started cross-examining me, and I said, "Well, major, I've been on guard duty, and I was told it was Army regulation that when you are on guard duty you didn't have to pull any type of regular duty." He asked me where I had taken my basic training and I said, "Fort McLellan, Alabama; most recently from the 3rd Infantry Division." That cured him! The major pulled duty in Iceland during the war, and had never seen a bit of combat.

Shortly thereafter they found that I could type a little, and they asked me to serve as a clerk in the Company Headquarters. I didn't particularly like that. My typing wasn't all that good, so I got a pass to Copenhagen, Denmark. I went up there with a fellow named Sipe. We had a most enjoyable time for about 10 days. I still have some souvenirs, and my meal ticket because we didn't eat too much in the Army facilities up there, except breakfast. There were a lot of guys who went with us to Denmark, and one lone black soldier. He was in the same compartment with us on the train. We got along all right.

Some of the guys told him that he might be going to Denmark, but not to fraternize with the white women. This black didn't pay any attention to them, and he found a white girl. As we were going back to Berlin, I noticed that he had a lot of bruises on him. It seemed that he found a white gal, and went into one of the nightclubs, and got the stew beat out of him. As I recall in Denmark it was very cold in January, and I could hardly stand up due to the icy streets and sidewalks. The old people were going around on ice skates, as well as the little kids. They seemed to be at ease, and skated along anywhere.

We met a couple of nice girls. We went out to their house and met their parents. We were sitting around in the living room, talking, and they offered me a Hershey bar. They didn't know that I didn't like Hershey bars, because of my experience in eating the chocolate D bars. I ate too many of them and had gotten sick, and for a long time I detested the taste of chocolate. (It's been only in the most recent years that I will eat some chocolate.) They pulled out a Hershey bar, and it looked like a brand new bar that hadn't been opened, and they wanted me to open it up and eat it. I said, "No, thank you. I don't really want it. I don't like chocolate." They didn't understand and kept insisting. I unwrapped it, thinking it was a Hershey bar, put it in my mouth, and took a bite. It was nothing but a piece of wood that had been worked on, and was in the exact shape of a Hershey bar. It looked like the "real thing." They really got a big kick out of it. I let them enjoy their little joke. We went out with these girls a couple of times, bade them good-bye, and came back to Berlin.

CHAPTER 22
GOING BACK TO THE STATES

It wasn't too long before we got orders that we were going back to the States.

Before I get into that, I'd like to show you the conditions in Berlin. I sent my basic pay home, except for the amount I spent at the PX for candy and cigarettes. For pastime, we played poker and shot dice, and you didn't care whether you won or not, because money wasn't any good. You could go out and sell a carton of cigarettes for 200 dollars. You could sell a candy bar for five dollars. You could get your clothes washed for five dollars. There was a widow across the street who had a young boy; she took in washing. She did a good job and she kept our clothes washed up, and we'd pay her about five dollars, and that was fine enough. The little boy would come around and pick up the clothes and bring them back to us. Berlin was one of the most enjoyable times of my career in the Army. We had plenty of good food to eat and not much duty. However, long toward the end, they started getting young recruits in from the States, and they started having to get strict with them. They started having reveille, and I wouldn't fall out for reveille. The old platoon sergeant used to get so exasperated with me. He'd say, "Craft, come on, you're going to get me in trouble." I would reply, "Aw, the hell with it. I'm not over here playing soldier. I want to go home." That was about it, on up until the latter part of March, when we were given these orders to move to another assembly area.

We stayed there several days or about a week and got on some cattle cars that didn't have seats. We rode to Bremmerhaven, got off there and stayed a few days. We were processed and boarded on the little SS *Antioch,* which held about 1,000 men. It took us about 12 days to come back across the ocean. We came back through the North Atlantic. That was in the first part of April, or around the middle of the month. It was an exciting experience because there were very high waves, and the waves would go 75 feet in the air, or higher. The ship would run up on one of those waves, raising up on its bow, and then the water would come down making a loud noise. It seemed as if the ship was going to jar apart. Out of sheer boredom, I volunteered for KP one time. I helped cook the meals. Then I was asked if I'd help wash down the steps of the deck. In a heavy storm and all that turbulence, the ship raised so much cain that I got seasick and had to quit and lie down. It didn't last long. I didn't volunteer for KP any more. I really had a good time. There were a lot of my old buddies that transferred out of the 3rd Division to the 78th Division with me. However, most of them were Yankees, and they had what they called a music room. There were boxes along the ship, where you could request songs. The favorite song of mine was "Sentimental Journey." My Yankee friends detested country music. They were always calling me rebel, so I'd place songs in the boxes that were of country music origin and sign their names to the request. They never did find out who was doing this. They'd say, "Well, who in the hell did that? I didn't request that song. I can't stand that crud." I'd listen to it and was smiling inside to myself. They never found out who did it.

Coming back on the ship, they were shooting craps. I reached the point where I liked to play poker, and I'd do it as a pastime over there. I told myself, that when I got home, I was never going to play any more. I didn't want it to get in my blood. I'm not a gambler. There was a guy named Hitchcock, from Batesville, Mississippi. He was from a little town, south of Memphis, and he liked to gamble. When we left Berlin, I had had 1,000 dollars in marks in my pocket. I traded 800 of them for 40 dollars. Hitchcock wanted to borrow the 40 dollars. I let him have it and was afraid that I wasn't going to get it back, but the old boy paid me before we got off the ship. It seemed like an eternity coming back, because that ship was so slow.

When we pulled into the New York harbor, the Red Cross had some pretty gals that came out on a tug boat, and they were singing some popular music along with "Sentimental Journey" welcoming us back. None of us respected the Red Cross, whom we believed was responsible for this welcome. We lined the decks and gave them a good booing. Those poor girls sat out there and sang in spite of the booing and ignored us.

Finally, we docked and got off. As we were moving towards the troop train to take us to Camp Kilmer, we met some Germans going back to Germany, who were prisoners. This was in April, 1946. We gave them a few cat calls, and remarked that those poor devils didn't know what they were getting into, because it wasn't the same Germany they had left. We continued on to Camp Kilmer, New Jersey, and as custom was, the Army gave us a steak dinner. I mean they went all out. They really had a good steak dinner. We thoroughly enjoyed it, but we couldn't eat all of it, because we weren't accustomed to that kind of food. Even the Coca-Cola tasted delicious, because cokes in Germany weren't as good. They didn't have the same flavor or taste. We stayed in Camp Kilmer for several days, and we were waiting to be processed. Some were trying to call home. I didn't try to call my parents, because I wanted to slip in unannounced. On a Wednesday night, we left Camp Kilmer about 6:00 p.m. on troop trains. When we left our barracks, there was a major with us. We enlisted men were allowed one duffel bag packed full of our clothes, belongings, and souvenirs.

And, incidentally, before I forget it, when we were in Salzburg, Austria, Lieutenant Katz, our platoon leader, along with other higher ranked men, found a warehouse full of Minox (spy) cameras that the Germans used. They were made in Latvia. They gave each officer three of them. Our platoon lieutenant gave Sergeant Greene and myself one, and kept one for himself. While I was in Salzburg, we had gone out on a march and upon my return, my gold watch I was going to bring home for my daddy was stolen.

From that day on, I carried my little Minox camera around in my field jacket pocket. One day, I stooped over, and the camera fell out. It didn't break the lens, but it cracked the viewer. But that didn't impair it. Other than a pistol, a 32 Watham, and some more souvenirs (I picked up some coins), stuff I'd picked up in Germany, Denmark and France, that's about all I brought back.

But this major had three duffel bags and a trunk full of stuff. He was loaded down. He was trying to carry all of it. He looked at us as if to say, "Fellows, won't you help me?" and we didn't even let on like we saw him. I don't know how he got his belongings to the train. We did not help him. I don't know if he was put on the train, because I never did see him again. We rode the troop train down through Virginia, and Tennessee, and somewhere in east Tennessee, we stopped at a little place with a store that sold ice cream nearby. Some of the guys kept saying, "I'd like some ice cream." I said, "I would, too." I jumped off the train, went in, handed the guy a five dollar bill; the train started moving. I grabbed my ice cream and told him to keep the change. I headed back and they pulled me on to the train, while it was moving.

We finally got to Camp Shelby the following Saturday about midnight. On Sunday morning, we were up getting processed, and they told us that we were going to get out at 9:00 a.m. on Monday morning. On that Sunday afternoon, I was lying on my bed; I had never pulled my dog-tags off since Fort McLellan. But that afternoon, I had taken a shower, and I lost the dog-tags in the barracks somewhere. I couldn't find them. We were all sitting around, shooting the bull and somebody said, "Craft, they are calling you on the loud speaker, and saying that you are wanted in the day room." I replied, "I didn't hear it. What could they want me for?" They said, "Well, you'd better go up there and find out." I didn't know what was going on, and I went up and immediately saw my dad. He'd come down with my brother-in-law and a neighbor to see me. It seems like the principal of one of the schools saw my name in the paper, that I had landed in New York, and was on my way to Camp Shelby, and would be there Saturday night and on Sunday. Dad and I had a joyful reunion and he left. The next day, I got on a bus and rode to Mount Olive. I thought that I could get a cab. I was told that it was possible, but I couldn't.

I started walking out on the highway. I'd crossed the railroads tracks on Highway 35, and a man came through with an old stripped down pickup. He stopped, backed up his truck and offered to give me a ride home, where I met my folks and we had a very joyful reunion.

That night, Willard Clark's parents came over with a bunch of neighbors. I had to relate the story of Willard's death all over again. It was very, very upsetting to me. However, I don't think they realized that. This became so frequent with the people dropping in to welcome me home, that mother and dad finally had to ask them not to talk to me any more about the war. I was very thankful for that.

I will say this: I wouldn't take anything for my experiences in the service in defending my country. It was a very hazardous situation. My life was in danger many, many times and I saw a lot of people killed, wounded and maimed, and, no doubt, I helped put away a few Germans. I don't know how many. I didn't keep notches on my gun, but I was glad to be able to say that I had served my country.

This concludes my tenure in World War II.

RETURN TO EUROPE

The last week of August, 1984, my wife and I decided to go to Europe and retrace my combat steps. When we arrived at Le Haute Jacques, we were greeted by the hostess, Jackie Bedel who gave us a warm reception.

During our stay we met Commandant Robert Renard who was very interested in the details of this great battle, and requested me to give him a copy of Fedela to Berchtesgaden, the Seventh Infantry narration of the war. He translated the chapter on the battle for Le Haute Jacques in French and posted it in 14 surrounding towns, for the people to read in order for them to understand the many sacrifices the Seventh Infantry had made in order to liberate this small place. The Commandant felt that they should replace the crude wooden plaque with better and more permanent monument.

He raised the money from the villages, with only one protest from the mayor of Taintrux who refused to cooperate. The people of Taintrux over-rode their mayor and organized their own campaign to raise money for the monument.

Commandant Renard employed an architect, who erected the monument. I was asked to come over on November 5, 1985 and unveil it. Betty went with me and we were the honored guests for that day. They prepared a feast which lasted more than four hours.

We were house guests of Commandant Renard and his wife, Suzanne, for a week.

EPILOGUE

It has been very difficult for me to write this book, as I had to relive the Agony of Hell. This was intended to be written at the request of my sons and daughter, in order that our children and grandchildren would have some idea of what war is all about.

This book is dedicated in memory of Willard Clark and my friends, Truett Thornton and Lee L. Dees, who were killed by the fanatical, criminal-minded, dastardly hired killers of Adolph Hitler, the Nazi maniac, who thought he could conquer the world. It was by the grace of God and prayers of my Christian parents that brought me through this horrible ordeal.

In order to tell this story, it was necessary to use the unsavory language of the infantry soldier, which has been toned down considerably. My hope is that there will be no more wars, but knowing there will be to the end of time, perhaps it will give some insight to the youngsters that will have to fight for their country.

May God continue to bless America and let Freedom ring. I am dedicated to the idea, when the signs of tyranny appear, that I will speak out and let my voice be heard.

My thanks to my lovely wife, Betty, who has given so much of her time in writing this book, and especially for her encouragement.

With the exception of my dearest friends, all from Smith County, Sergeant White, and Johnny T. Clayton, all the names have been changed, and any similarity to persons living or dead is purely coincidental.

Printed in the USA
CPSIA information can be obtained
at www.ICGtesting.com
JSHW082228140824
68134JS00016B/781